John Milton the Elder and His Music

NUMBER TWO OF THE
COLUMBIA UNIVERSITY STUDIES
IN MUSICOLOGY

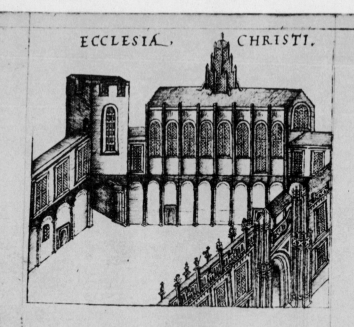

ECCLESIA, CHRISTI.

Prima stat australis Domus ampla, Ecclesia Christi,
  Primo iam duplici nomine digna loco.
Tùm quia te, patremq; tuum sit nacta patronum,
  Tùm quia sit reliquis author ista cohors.
Cœpta quidem Thomæ Wulsei sumptibus olim,
  Sed patris Henrici censibus aucta tui.

Cœpit sub Henrico octauo. per Thomam Wulsæum } Anno dñi. 1529.
Archiepiscopum Eboracensem. absoluta est ab eodem } Anno dñi. 1546.
Henrico octauo.

CHRIST CHURCH, ABOUT 1566

By *ERNEST BRENNECKE, Jr.*

John Milton the Elder
and His Music

New York: Morningside Heights

COLUMBIA UNIVERSITY PRESS
MCMXXXVIII

THE COLUMBIA UNIVERSITY COUNCIL FOR RESEARCH
IN THE HUMANITIES AND THE AMERICAN COUNCIL OF
LEARNED SOCIETIES HAVE GENEROUSLY CONTRIBUTED
FUNDS TO ASSIST IN THE PUBLICATION OF THIS VOLUME

To

THE REVEREND DR. ERNEST BRENNECKE

"Nunc mea Pierios cupiam per pectora fontes
Irriguas torquere vias, totumque per ora
Volvere laxatum gemino de vertice rivum;
Ut tenues oblita sonos audacibus alis
Surgat in officium venerandi Musa parentis."

Ioannis Miltoni, *Ad Patrem*, 1-5

Preface

TO BE KNOWN to posterity solely as the parent of an illustrious child is a destiny that doubtless has its attractions. It is not, however, the most enviable of all possible fates. And John Milton, the poet's father (as he is invariably identified), might have felt his natural pride crossed by an excusable twinge of chagrin had he foreseen his present position in the estimation of the world.

Many students of poetry, to be sure, honor him for his sheer luck with his son and namesake; they respect him for his ability in the most prosaic of literary pursuits, the drawing up of legal documents; they envy him his financial success as a real estate operator; they commend him for providing his offspring with an excellent education and an impeccable moral upbringing; they even detect a glimmer of artistic talent in his affection for organ music and psalm singing. His own "psalm tunes" are often mentioned as if they were his only musical compositions, but it is interesting to note that although he harmonized several such tunes, he never actually invented any in his life, so far as we know. But his extended musical works, of which a fair number survive, have been widely disregarded.

That relatively little attention has been bestowed upon his larger achievements seems strange, in view of the extraordinarily close and affectionate relationship that is known to have existed between him and his celebrated son for almost forty years. Many features of the poet Milton's personality, many of his tastes, opinions, and accomplishments, may receive enhanced understanding when viewed as the results of his unusual intimacy with his richly gifted father.

Preface

From the early lyric, *At a Solemn Music,* to the characteriza-
tion of Manoa in *Samson,* the works of the poet, in both prose
and verse, abound in passages that demand familiarity with the
elder Milton and his music. Specifically, the important poem
Ad Patrem receives its full measure of appreciation only when
it is read in its proper setting, that is, against the background of a
knowledge of the poet's filial relationships. Furthermore, a
study of the father's character and eventful career may show
how closely the son's accomplishments were, in several senses,
understandable offshoots of the artistic splendors of the age of
Elizabeth and Shakespeare.

Possibly the elder Milton's preoccupation with music has thus
far preserved him from the keener scrutiny of students of literature. But the small amount of trouble that an examination of his
compositions entails does surely and greatly reward the investi-
gator. It is not surprising, at any rate, that a handful of musical
antiquarians have indeed conceded to him, in his own right, a
position of some eminence in their art. They know that he made
ambitious contributions to a few famous publications of his time.
Some of them have taken the trouble to examine, and even to
hear, the more accessible of his works, and have noted with
surprise that he often lacks the stiff and clumsy touch that one
has every right to expect from an amateur.

But even these more generous critics do him less than justice.
The present essay sets out to show that the elder Milton was a
far more talented composer, a more daring and influential artist,
and a far more interesting human being than most of us have
fancied him to be. If we listen to his music today, it delivers to us
across the centuries an impression of a great personality, at once
genial, robust, and touchingly impassioned.

To this strong and appealing character the accidents of birth
have been doubly disadvantageous. He not only has sat through
the generations unnoticed in the colossal shadow cast by his son,

but he was also forced in his own time to compete as a musician with the most gifted composers who were active as a group at any time in England. It was his misfortune as well as his fortune to have been born into the late Tudor period, when extraordinary accomplishment was casually accepted as the sheerest commonplace in almost every branch of human effort; in warfare and poetry, in crime and philosophy, in corruption and chivalry, in amour and architecture, in adventure and music. That Tudor music more than holds its own with the rest of Tudor art and science scarcely needs saying. But its transcendent qualities are not yet popularly recognized.

When the casual reader of today thinks of the scores of passages in which Shakespeare describes the miraculous powers of organized sound, when he reads the songs in Elizabethan plays, just what sort of music passes through his mind's ear? "How sweet the moonlight sleeps upon this bank" . . . "Hark, hark, the lark" . . . do not these words invoke Chopin and Schubert? When he reads the younger Milton's glowing lines on organs and choir singing, "That undisturbed song of pure concent, Ay sung before the saphire-colour'd throne," is it not natural for him to think of Handel and Bach? It may be slightly disconcerting to reflect that even the genius of a Shakespeare or of a Milton could scarcely have stretched itself to know music that came into being a century or two after his body was dust. A further flash of logic carries us to the conviction that if our two greatest poets were unacquainted with the most ancient classics familiar to most modern listeners, they must have lived on intimate terms with music of some kind. Finally, it could not have been poor or crude music that transported them to such heights of eloquence.

And indeed it was not. A belated but ardent revival of Elizabethan music has now been carried on for more than a generation in the British Isles. It has enlisted the services of countless

professors, editors, instrument makers, publishers, singing societies, virtuosi, and orchestras. Gradually the thousands of
compositions that once enraptured Sir Philip Sidney, Sir Francis
Bacon, and Queen Elizabeth herself, and then collected silent
dust for almost three centuries, are opening a new and complex
world of enjoyment to ears that have begun to tire of the com-
parative naïvety of Strauss and Stravinsky. We are beginning
to comprehend the majestic powers of Tallis and Byrd in the
many-voiced motet, of John Bull and Giles Farnaby in scintil-
lating keyboard filigree, of Dowland and Pilkington in the
delicate air for voice and lute, of Gibbons and Weelkes in the anthem, of Morley and Wilbye in the madrigal. To each of these
names we could add ten more without approaching the end of
our roll call of accomplished masters.

In the embarrassing splendor of this company the elder Milton held a position that was far from humble. His work was
rated, and printed, with the best. He was a genius in his own
right long before he had any children. That, at least, is the thesis
of the present essay, a thesis which has emerged from a fresh
examination of contemporary documents and from the pleasant
labor of scoring and hearing all his music which is known to have
survived, in print or in manuscript. More than half of it has
hitherto been completely ignored. The story of his career, frag-
mentary and obscure as much of it is, brings us into contact with
the characteristic intellectual color and humor of the age of
Gloriana and James. An analysis of the music itself, ranging
from the simple to the architecturally complicated and grandiose,
from deep pathos and lamentation to the most winning frivolity,
should dissipate the notion that a dabbling tinkerer or a dour
puritan was here at work.

The present writer entertains some hope that his effort will
have more than a sentimental appeal to students of the younger
Milton, since it throws a number of new details into the picture

of the poet's artistic environment. He prays also that he may hereby help to instigate some actual performances of music that still holds more than antiquarian value. With a small amateur choir he presented a little of it before the English Graduate Union, at Columbia University, in the autumn of 1934. On that occasion he became convinced that such performances may win a long overdue appreciation for the gifted artist whose bad luck (in a sense) it was to beget the author of *Paradise Lost*.

For the convenience of the general reader who wishes to run through the biographical narrative as comfortably as possible, the necessary critical and technical apparatus has been relegated to the footnotes. These notes, together with their references to the Bibliography and the collection of musical examples in score, will guide the critical reader, whether his specialty is music or literature, to all of the writer's sources of information.

Chapter I, narrating the events of a single typical day, is an attempt to show in detail how Milton as a boy was probably subjected to those influences which were to sway him most powerfully as an artist. Its narrative method seemed to the writer to be the most efficient as well as pleasurable means of communicating the necessary background to the reader. But it is less fictional than it might seem, since it contains no statement made without some foundation of plausibility. It has already appeared, without its footnotes, in *Music and Letters* (London) of January, 1938. The writer feels confident that his readers will recognize it as compounded of both actual and typical events, and he trusts that they will not find too disagreeable the task of distinguishing between the two forms of truth. These observations apply partially to a few additional passages for which no firmer foundation than mere plausibility can be supplied, such as the circumstances of the "Oriana" project, in Chapter III, and of Milton's associations with his contemporaries, particularly in Chapter IV. There is, of course, the possibility that the future discovery of fresh material will modify the pictures here painted. But there is little likelihood that their main outlines will be radically altered.

For invaluable assistance in the preparation of this essay the writer is chiefly indebted to Professor Frank A. Patterson, general editor of the definitive Columbia edition of the younger Milton's complete works, who is largely responsible for whatever virtues are to be found here (but not for any errors of fact or judgment); to Professor Paul H. Láng, whose experience in the music of the period enabled him to supply invaluable suggestions; to Professor Nelson G. McCrea and the Council on Research in the Humanities, and to the American Council of Learned Societies, for subventions which greatly lightened the financial burden of the undertaking for both author and publisher; to the Director and Trustees of the British Museum, the Governors of Dulwich College, the Bodleian Library, and the Governing Body of Christ Church, Oxford, for permission to use and reproduce important source documents; to the members of the Choir of Trinity Lutheran Church, of New York, who have displayed remarkable enthusiasm and virtuosity in the difficult task of singing Milton's music.

E. B., Jr.

Columbia University
March 1, 1938

Contents

I. A DAY AT CHRIST CHURCH, 1573   3

II. OXFORD AND THE POLISH PRINCE (1573-
1585)   25

III. LONDON AND ORIANA (1585-1603)   44

IV. LAMENTATIONS OF A SORROWFUL SOUL
(1603-1614)   61

V. THE REMEDY FOR SADNESS (1615-1618)   80

VI. THE WHOLE BOOK OF PSALMS (1618-1624)   94

VII. FATHER AND SON (1624-1638)   112

VIII. REMAINING WORKS AND LAST YEARS
(1638-1647)   136

MILTON'S EXTANT MUSIC; A CHRONOLOGICAL LIST   153

BIBLIOGRAPHY   154

EXAMPLES OF MUSIC   163

INDEX   213

Illustrations

Christ Church, about 1566, after Bereblock; Bodl. MS 13, f.5ᵛ

Frontispiece

A document witnessed and signed by Milton as scrivener   50

Title page from the Cantus Book "The Triumphes of Oriana"   54

Tenor part of Milton's "Fair Orian"   58

Title page of Leighton's "Teares or Lamentacions"   72

Milton's "Thou God of Might"   76

Title page of Myriell's "Tristitiae remedium"   82

Sextus part of Milton's "Precamur"   86

The Elder Milton's sonnet to John Lane   92

End of Preface and List of Composers of Ravenscroft's Psalter   102

Milton's setting of Psalm 27   106

Court order exonerating Milton of charges of fraud   132

Tenor part of Milton's "In Nomine"   142

John Milton the Elder and His Music

CHAPTER I

A Day at Christ Church

1573

IT WAS a few minutes before five o'clock of a November morning in the fifteenth year of the reign of our Sovereign Lady Elizabeth. The seven-ton bell, Great Tom, in the tower of St. Frideswide's Cathedral Church was tolling lustily.[1] "In Thomae laude resono Bim Bom sine fraude" was the jocular legend it bore. This ponderous whimsy was probably wasted upon some hundred and thirty servants, students, and officers of Christ Church, whom it summoned to the College prayers. They trooped shivering into the bleak Norman edifice, whose 144-foot spire had dominated the town and the University of Oxford since the thirteenth century.

John Piers, the dean himself, and the eight canons of the Corporation, gowned and hooded, were already in their stalls. The students hastily assembled, knowing that fines would be exacted without mercy for laxity in attendance. The chaplains were ready to begin.[2] Master William Blitheman,[3] chafing his

[1] The bell came originally from Oseney Abbey. It now hangs in Tom Tower, built by Wren in 1682. Thompson, pp. 229; 251. Henry Lawes, friend of the younger Milton, wrote an interesting round for three voices to the words, "Great Tom is cast, and Christ Church bells ring 1, 2, 3, 4, 5, 6, and Tom comes last"; also a catch for four voices, "Well Rung, Tom, Boy." See the Euterpe Round Book, Oxford University Press, No. 29, pp. 13, 22.

[2] For details as to the organization and personnel of the college and cathedral, see Thompson, pp. 12, 34, 36.

[3] There is fairly persuasive evidence that Blitheman was at this time master of the Christ Church choristers. For concise biographical details, see Grove. He may have been assisted by an organist, Bartholomew Lant, about whom extremely little is known. See West, p. 84.

3

hands before the organ, glanced over to see whether the sixteen singers in his choir were there, gave a nod to the boy who plied the bellows, and sounded G, the reciting note. The officiating priest lifted up his voice and intoned the opening sentence: "When the wicked man turneth away from the wickedness that he hath committed, and doeth that which is lawful and right, he shall save his soul alive. . . ." [4]

He proceeded with the Exhortation; presently all fell to their knees on the stone pavement and repeated the Confession after him, phrase by phrase: "We have erred, and strayed from thy ways like lost sheep. . . ." There followed the Absolution and the Lord's Prayer, in monotone. Master Blitheman then sounded the deeper note C, and the priest chanted, "O Lord, open thou our lips." The choir responded, "And our mouth shall show forth thy praise," in the broad and magnificent harmonies contrived a few years before by Master Thomas Tallis, of the Queen's Majesty's Chapel—harmonies which are still to be heard in every English Cathedral Church on great festivals. [5]

For the first of the canticles, the Venite Exultemus, and the psalms for the day, the music was so familiar that the eight lay clerks and the eight boys in choir stalls scarcely needed to glance at their notes. But while the first lesson was being read, they nervously fingered their service books. Presently they would have to sing more exacting compositions, and any inattentive slips would call for chastisement later in the day. Some distinguished London musicians were visiting Oxford at this time, and for their benefit Master Blitheman had arranged that the

[4] Ordinary services at Christ Church were probably in English, although on special occasions Latin, Greek, or Hebrew might have been used, in accordance with the provisions of the Act of Uniformity of 1549 and of Royal Letters Patent of 1560. In this respect the college chapels of the two universities were specially privileged. See Wooldridge (1) p. 207n.

[5] Tallis's "festal" responses have been many times reprinted; e.g., in Jebb, I, 6; Boyce, I, 1; *Cathedral Prayer Book*, Appendix, p. 2.

choral portions of this service were to be a little more elaborate than was usual on a weekday.

The boy choristers had got out of bed at four o'clock that morning. They had danced for warmth on the rush-covered floor, had slipped hastily into breeches and shirts, had breakfasted very frugally on porridge, and had donned their little white surplices. They were not particularly aware of the fact that they were undergoing any great hardship. As children of relatively humble station they could count themselves fortunate in receiving gentlemen's educations. Some of them were even then being equipped for meritorious careers. One of these was named John Milton.[6] He was at this time about ten years old.[7]

This Milton had come from the little agricultural parish of Stanton St. John, less than five miles to the northeast of Oxford itself. His father, Richard Milton,[8] was a yeoman, or almost-gentleman farmer, who had inherited a small property in 1561. The class to which he belonged has been regarded with reason as the backbone of British society. Since its members were not above working with their hands, they were not officially recognized as gentlefolk. But they enjoyed immense advantages over the poorer tenant farmers, laborers, menials, and hirelings of all kinds. They were economically independent; they had a voice

[6] There is no reason for suspecting Aubrey's much discussed statement: "He [the elder Milton] was brought up in the University of Oxon, at Christ Church," although the university records, which were carelessly kept, tell us nothing of his presence. Masson places his Oxford career between 1577 and 1582, but there is every reason to suppose that the boy had come to Christ Church as early as 1572. His training both as a boy chorister and as a student would account most satisfactorily for the known details of his later career. For all the available evidence, see Masson, Vol. I; Arkwright (Memoir), p. 4; Pulver; Bridge, pp. 65-68. Bridge, however, gives his birth date wrongly as 1553.

[7] There is little doubt but that Milton was born in 1563. His son Christopher, in an affidavit of April, 1637, declared that his father was then aged about 74 years; see p. 131.

[8] All the known details concerning Richard as well as the more remote ancestors of Milton are fully discussed in Masson, I, 7-40.

in the local government. Above all, their chances of bettering their condition were considerable, given a bit of enterprise and luck. They could acquire wealth, fine clothes, and servants. They could build themselves large houses; they could command a tolerant respect from the local gentry. With increasing prosperity they might eventually aspire to win a crest and to insinuate their families gradually into the ranks of polite or even idle society.

Such was apparently the aim of Richard Milton, although it must be admitted that his progress had not been phenomenally speedy as yet. He may have married ambitiously, selecting his wife from a family of higher social standing than his own—but her identity has never been established. It was in the education of his son John, perhaps his only child, that his ambitions found more genuine exercise. His first step was probably to send the boy, while still an infant, to some impoverished but at least literate man or woman in the parish. Under such a person, the shabby mistress of a "dame school" or a broken down scholar, the child may have worked with his hornbook, learned his ABC's, the Lord's Prayer, and an abbreviated catechism. He might even have gained a smattering of the Latin Gloria and Creed and the rudiments of penmanship. In time, he might read portions of the Bible and shudder deliciously over Fox's *Acts and Monuments*. But here his schooling could readily have ended, for even the most prosperous yeoman in the tiny parish could scarcely have afforded to place his son in a good public school.

It was nothing less than a master stroke to get the boy admitted as a chorister of Christ Church. Fortune undoubtedly played into Richard's hands, offering a beautiful combination of circumstances: the proximity of the town, the very center of elegant art and learning; the vacant place in a first-class choir; young John's at least passable voice. His education was assured for a number of years at least, without expense, since the *pueri musici* were maintained at the cost of the Foundation. And the possibilities for advancement thereafter were almost limitless. Had not the former dean of Christ Church, Thomas Cooper himself, begun as a chorister of Magdalen College and risen as a Fellow, as a celebrated lexicographer, as master of the School, and was he not now already Bishop of Lincoln? Richard might well have been more than pleased, as he administered his slowly growing property, to think of his son's association with the mighty doctors of the Church and of the university.

But there in the cathedral the time was approaching for the singing of the Te Deum. John opened his book: "Mornyng and Evenyng Praier and Communion, set forthe in foure partes, to be sung in Churches, both for Men and Children, with dyvers other Godly praiers & anthems of sundry men's doings. . . ." This book[9] had appeared eight years before, and contained the most useful church music of the time. The canticles to be sung on this occasion were by Thomas Causton, a gentleman of the Chapel Royal, who had died in 1569.[10] His work was almost simple enough to satisfy the royal injunction that "a modest and distinct song" was to be so used that it might be "understood as if it were read without singing," [11] and it was at the same time elaborate and eloquent enough to appeal to the tastes of learned musicians.

[9] This compilation was a second and amplified edition of the first important collection of choral music, printed in 1560, for the reformed English rite: John Day's *Certaine Notes* "set forthe in foure and three partes, to be sung at the Mornyng, Communion and Evenyng Praier, very necessarie for the Church of Christe to be frequented and used: and unto them be added divers Godly Praiers & Psalms in the like forme to the honour & prayse of God. Imprinted at London, over Aldersgate, beneath S. Martin's, by John Day." See Bumpus, I, 14-17.

[10] Causton's three Services (Morning, Communion, and Evening) are most conveniently available in the excellent modern editions by Royle Shore: The Cathedral Series of Church Service Music; London, Novello; Nos. 2 (1933), 3, and 4 (1912).

[11] See Procter, p. 59.

7

A chaplain with a resonant bass voice delivered the opening verse in florid plainsong: "We praise thee, O God," and the full choir boldly threw its voices into massive harmonies that echoed from the wooden ceiling: "We knowledge thee to be the Lord. All the earth doth worship thee. . . ." The sound gathered intensity, reaching a sonorous climax with the words, "the Father everlasting," when the lower voices clashed into discords and blended again into consonance. The music sank to a whisper: "Holy, holy, Lord God of Sabaoth," and then surged on in mounting waves.

After a dramatic pause, young Milton and his companions in the treble part led off alone with the phrase, "Thine honorable, true, and only Son." They were imitated successively by the altos, then by the tenors, and finally by the basses, reveling in the mysterious effects of accent created by syncopation, especially when the note E, sung by Milton, was followed by the basses singing E-flat, producing the most discordant of all possible musical intervals. Such moments were to be relished and treasured, as Milton already understood. This was not precisely a "modest and distinct song," but only insensitive ears and minds could resist its powerful appeal to the feelings. So the canticle proceeded, with further and more vigorous imitations, with solid blocks of harmony, with ingenious interweavings of the parts, with monotonous but emotional cadences, to the last sentence, "Let me never be confounded," wherein a daring harmony was at last resolved into a gentle expiring chord. Master Blitheman nodded his approval.

After the second Lesson, Causton's Benedictus was sung, a composition in the same style, in which Milton, with the trebles, three times emphasized the melody of the ancient Tonus Peregrinus. Even though this solemn tune here carried English words and was embedded in a mass of counterpoint, it was recognized by all the older worshippers as part of their artistic heritage from the mediaeval Church. At the concluding words, "World without end. Amen," the whole choir executed complicated rising leaps and falling scales, finishing with rather dazzling brilliance. Again it was here demonstrated that the musicians, though they might be irreproachable Elizabethan Protestants, could not readily abandon the beauties, both ornate and severe, that had been developed by their papist ancestors.

There was, to be sure, no lack of precisionist opposition to such elaborate renditions of Divine Service. Only one year before this, Thomas Cartwright had published his scathing invective against such Romish profanation.[12] "They toss the Psalms in most places," he wrote, "like tennis balls. . . . As for organs and curious singing, though they be proper to Popish dens, I mean to cathedral churches, yet some others also must have them. The Queen's chapel, and these churches (which should be spectacles of Christian reformation) are rather patterns and precedents to the people of all superstition." Such protests were common enough, but fortunately they were seldom heeded by the more powerful ecclesiastical organizations.

When the Benedictus was concluded, the whole congregation arose and chanted the Apostles' Creed in plainsong. Then followed the usual versicles and responses, while all knelt, and the prayers. An anthem was next appointed, for "Quires and Places where they sing," according to the innocently ironical instruction in the Prayer Book. For this day the anthem was also found in John Day's *Mornyng and Evenyng Praier;* it was Tallis's *If Ye Love Me, Keep My Commandments.*[13] It had already been sung many times here at Christ Church, and the boy Milton had become aware of its tranquil devotional quality; he had been taught to admire the easy skill of its composer, especially where the sustained tones swelled out and subsided as one voice gently

---

[12] Hawkins, I, 457n.
[13] Republished by Novello, "The Musical Times Series," No. 231. See p. 138.

overlapped another with the words, "that he may abide with you for ever"—and when the quiet last section was repeated, note for note, as though the mood of the moment were to be abandoned only with great reluctance. Milton was destined one day to write a remarkably similar setting of the same text.

After the last notes of the anthem had died away, prayers were said, the supplication for "our most gracious Sovereign Lady, Queen Elizabeth," being repeated with particular fervency, and the Pauline Benediction brought the service to a close. A considerable portion of the worshippers remained, however, to hear Master Blitheman play an outgoing voluntary[14] of his own composition upon the organ, for his prowess at the keyboard was well known. And so the grave old Dorian melody, *Gloria tibi Trinitas* soared aloft, ornamented by sparkling runs which were executed by the organist's agile left hand.[15] The runs presently gave away to the novelty of double notes and syncopated rhythms. When he had finished, a little group of admiring connoisseurs gathered around him.

It was now nearly six o'clock, and Milton had to tear himself away. After removing his surplice, he hurried across the great quadrangle with his companions, perhaps shying a clod or two at a stray pig wallowing in the autumnal mud. He would not have to take part in the daily Communion Service at the cathedral; instead, he was now to be subjected to two hours of nonmusical schooling. A few moments later found him sitting on a long wooden form in a small room. The Master entered; the boys rose and piped together, "Salve, magister!" "Salvete, pueri; estote salvi!" was the grave reply, and all were ready for the business of the day. The Master opened his book, *Liber precum ecclesiae cathedralis Christi Oxon*, the official elementary work of instruction and devotion, which was to remain in

[14] For the use of organ voluntaries in early services, see Jebb, II, 18.
[15] Blitheman's composition is printed in Rimbault, pp. 237-239.

use there for almost three hundred years more.[16] It contained a psalter, a catechism, and prayers.

Portions of these were duly recited from memory by the boys, who were expected to remain letter perfect in them. Then came intensive exercises in Latin—grammar, reading, and composition. Unlucky was the boy who wrote a wrong inflection or read a false quantity. The Master's birch rod was seldom spared for him. But such chastisement was accepted by the pupils as an entirely normal and inevitable portion of the daily routine. In this way they learned the severe moral lessons in their elementary conversation book, the *Sententiae pueriles*,[17] and they were making some slight headway into the hexameters of Virgil, the odes of Horace, and the elegant prose of Cicero. Thereafter they were lectured and drilled in the manners becoming to learned and humble gentlemen and received praise or punishment appropriate to their behavior during the preceding four-and-twenty hours.

From this elevating regimen Milton was released at eight o'clock, feeling that the most trying part of the day was now over. He proceeded to the somewhat larger room, where there was "a pair of organs" [18] and where Master Blitheman now awaited his pupils for the daily lesson in instrumental playing. Blitheman found it possible to be an unusually kind and patient teacher as well as a Godfearing man and a musical virtuoso. He lavished especial sympathy upon his poorer scholars.[19] With

[16] See Thompson, p. 37.

[17] Davis, p. 115. For the similar training of the choir boys of St. George's Chapel, Windsor, at this period, see *Tudor Church Music*, X, 156.

[18] The expression, "pair of organs," common at this time (cf. "pair of virginals"), meant only a single instrument. The large organ in the cathedral was probably a single-manual instrument, without pedals, with four stops: diapasons, principal (sounding the upper octave), and possibly a reed. The smaller organs, used for practice, were portable or semiportable. See Galpin, pp. 215-237; and *The Musical Antiquary*, October, 1912, pp. 20-30.

[19] Blitheman's epitaph, at one time above his burial place in St. Nicholas Olave's

Milton in the little group of eager students this morning might have been John Bull, also ten years of age, who was later to become one of the most brilliant keyboard performers and composers in the world.[20]

Milton was called upon first to play a very brief composition, called *A Poynte*, by Blitheman's friend, John Shepherd.[21] He was shown how its four lines of melody, written just as a choir would sing them, could be brought out distinctly by making clever use of his thumbs, a device which Blitheman was fond of exploiting and which former players had scarcely thought of using. The boy took so readily to his lesson that he was promised permission to accompany the choristers in the chapel before very long. More advanced pupils then performed a *Voluntary*, by

---

Church, Queenhithe, is an interesting document, even if its laudatory sentiments must be slightly discounted. Pulver quotes it in full:

> Here Blitheman lies, a worthy wight
> Who feared God above;
> A friend to all a Foe to none,
> Whom Rich and Poore did love.
> Of Princes Chappell, gentleman,
> Unto his dying day;
> Whom all took great delight to heare
> Him on the Organs play.
> Whom passing Skill in Musick's Art,
> A Scholar left behind;
> John Bull (by name) his Master's veine,
> Expressing in each kinde.
> But nothing here continues long,
> No resting Place can have;
> His Soule departed hence to Heaven,
> His body here in Grave.

[20] Blitheman was certainly Bull's instructor, but the precise period at which the instruction took place is an exceedingly disputable point. The article in Grove says it took place in the Queen's Chapel, where Blitheman became organist in 1585 and Bull joint organist in 1588. But Bull was by that time a completely accomplished musician, having already been organist and master of the children at Hereford Cathedral. In the absence of any evidence to the contrary, the probability remains that Bull was one of Blitheman's pupils at Christ Church.

[21] This little piece was printed by Hawkins, II, 932.

Master Allwood,[22] and a *Meane*, by Master Blitheman.[23] All these compositions were played out of a big manuscript book compiled by Thomas Mulliner, who had been organist of Corpus Christi College and was later master of the choir of St. Paul's Cathedral.[24]

A couple of new boys were given much simpler exercises. Finally an exceptionally bright student, perhaps young Master Bull, played Blitheman's latest and most advanced piece, an *In Nomine*, in which the plainsong, *Gloria tibi Trinitas*, was ornamented both above and below with rapidly flowing triplets.[25] It was important, explained the master, for the organist's fingers to be able to play the notes that the choir would sing; but was not the organ worth hearing by itself? And if so, why not make it do more brilliant things than even the most agile voices could manage? He then told the boys how, on the continent of Europe, which he hoped they would one day visit, organs were already being built with not merely one but two manual keyboards and with an extra keyboard for the feet, which operated pipes that sang far more deeply and resonantly than the bass sections of the biggest choirs in the Kingdom. The time would come, he intimated, when works would be written for these instruments which would far outdo in splendor anything that had as yet been heard upon earth. He then left them to scrape on viols, strum on lutes, and pipe on recorders until eleven o'clock, when they proceeded to dinner.

The entire choir of the House gathered in a group at one end of the long refectory table, for "the old and laudable custom of

[22] *Ibid.*, II, 932-933.   [23] *Ibid.*, II, 931-932.

[24] Now in the British Museum (Add. MS. 30513). Probably the most important document for early Elizabethan keyboard music. See Davey, pp. 118-121; Walker, pp. 50-51; Van den Borren, pp. 16-21; Nagel, II, pp. 83-84. A complete list of its contents is in the *Catalogue of Manuscript Music in the British Museum*, III, 77-79.

[25] In *The Fitzwilliam Virginal Book*, I, 181-182. See Naylor (1), pp. 169, 177, 185, 207.

singing Grace in the Hall" was strictly maintained.[26] For some time the graces found in the *Liber precum* had been sung very simply in unison. But only two years before, a remarkable collection of choral songs, both secular and sacred (including "Grace before Meat" and "Grace after Meat"), by Thomas Whythorne, had been published in part books.[27] It was the only work of its kind printed between Wynkyn de Worde's book of 1530 and William Byrd's first book of madrigals of 1588. Master Blitheman had been strongly interested in it and had persuaded the dean and canons to permit portions of it to be used publicly at Christ Church.

And so, before the assembled scholars and masters fell upon their steaming dishes of meat, the choristers loudly sang Whythorne's bold setting of the words, "Almighty God, thy loving care is to provide for us alway. . . ."[28] All now dined bountifully upon beef, mutton, and poultry, using their pocket knives and their fingers, as custom demanded. Since the boys were under the eyes of their mentors in elegant deportment, they were careful not to pick their teeth with their knives, nor to blow their noses with the hand they had used upon the food. After the meal, Whythorne's second grace, "O our Father, we yield to thee," was sung.

For two hours after noon the boy choristers sat with their Latin tutors and diligently prepared for the morrow's recita-

---

[26] Cf. Thompson, p. 62.

[27] *Songes, for three, fower, and fiue voyces composed and made by Thomas Whythorne, Gent. the which songes be of sundry sortes, that is to say, some long, some short, some hard, some easie to be songe, and some betwene both: also some solemne, and some pleasant or mery: so that according to the skill of the singers (not being Musitians) and disposition and delite of the hearers, they may here finde songes for their contentation and liking. Now newly published An. 1571. At London, Printed by John Daye, dwelling over Aldersgate.* See Warlock (2); Grove; Walker, p. 58; Fellowes (1), pp. 34-36.

[28] "Grace before Meat" and "Grace after Meat," transcribed and edited (for modern use) by Peter Warlock. *Oxford Choral Songs from the Old Masters*, Oxford University Press, Nos. 358 and 359.

tions. They were then ready for a more serious session with Master Blitheman, who was taking them through a course of instruction which he properly called "practical music," although it would today be known as "theory."

He first required the youngest boys to recite their gamut, that is, the series of tones beginning with the bass G and extending to the treble E. It was not sufficient to name them merely by letter, for the entire range was divided into seven series, called hexachords, each of six notes denoted by the syllables *ut, re, mi, fa, sol, la.* These hexachords overlapped in a puzzling manner, so that each lettered note was distinguished by one, two, or three syllables. The lowest note was gamma-*(ut)* (whence the name gamut) and was followed by A-*(re)* and B-*(mi)*. The next note was C, the fourth step in the first hexachord and the first step in the second: C-*(Fa-ut)*. By the time the third hexachord was reached, the notes were called G-*(sol-re-ut)*, A-*(la-mi-re)*, and so on. Shakespeare's Hortensio, it will be remembered, declared his adoration of the matchless Bianca in the guise of a music master's gamut lesson:[29]

> Gam-ut I am, the ground of all accord,
> A-re, to plead Hortensio's passion;
> B-mi, Bianca, take him for thy lord,
> C-fa-ut, that loves with all affection:
> D-sol-re, one cliff, two notes have I:
> E-la-mi, show pity or I die.

This was no doubt a dry matter for healthy adolescents to learn by rote, but the lads took to it with suspicious eagerness. They knew well that the slightest slip might cost them real shillings and pence. For they took full advantage of the amusing custom of "spur money," an innocent form of graft.[30] Any gentleman who entered a cathedral during service wearing spurs, whose jingling supposedly created a disturbance, was not per-

---

[29] *Taming of the Shrew*, III, iii, 72.   [30] Bumpus, pp. 103-107.

mitted to leave without distributing small fees or fines to the choir boys. Immediately after the benediction he would be surrounded by the children, swarming about him "like so many white butterflies," as Dekker expressed it, and he would be forced to "quoit silver into the boys' hands." If he refused to do so, or if his purse was empty, the boys would make off with his hat, and he would have no redress. Since Christ Church was frequently visited by men of great position from all over the Kingdom, spur money was rather plentiful. The victim, if he was wise, might, however, save himself in one way. He was allowed to choose the youngest or stupidest looking chorister and require him to recite his gamut; and if the boy failed in a single syllable, no spur money could be exacted. The urchin who thus let his companions down would presently receive certain corrective treatment from them.

Next, the choristers were checked on their knowledge of "time" and "prolation," [31] having learned that in "perfect time" a breve note was equal to three semibreves, and in "imperfect time" to two semibreves. Likewise in the "greater prolation" a semibreve was equal to three minims, and in the "lesser prolation" to two minims. They had learned the symbols used to designate these time relationships. In addition, they were taught the more complicated matter of "proportions," the various rhythmic signs by which the apparent time values of the notes were altered. There were the "proportions of multiplicity," governing the ratio of short notes to long ones, from *dupla* (two against one) to *decupla* (ten against one); and the "proportions of inequality," applied to groups of equal notes with unequal ratio—the commonest of these were *sesquialtera* (three against two), *sesquitertia* (four against three), and *subsequitertia* (three against four), but there were many more.

[31] *Tudor Church Music*, I, xxxiv-xxxv. For further accounts of sixteenth century notation, see H. Bellerman, *Die Mensuralnoten und Taktzeichen des XV. und XVI. Jahrhunderts*, Berlin, 1906; and J. Wolf, *Handbuch der Notationskunde*, Vol. I, Berlin, 1913.

These were diligently studied, but even a professional musician could never hope to master the subject completely. As Thomas Morley said a few years later, "If a man would ingulf himself to learn to sing and set down all them which Franchinus Gaufurius hath set down in his book *De Proportionibus musicis,* he should find it a matter not only hard, but almost impossible." [32] To know the elements of the system, however, was essential, even for an amateur. Shakespeare's Richard II, even while awaiting death in the dungeon, could say, in the greatest irritation: [33]

> ... Music do I hear?
> Ha, ha! keep time. How sour sweet music is,
> When time is broke, and no proportion kept!

Again there was the matter of the modes, twelve in number, which correspond, with certain very vital differences, to the major and minor scales used in modern music. The boys were taught how melodies may begin, be inflected or modulated, and end, in the first, or Dorian, mode, resting on D; in the second, or Hypodorian; in the third, or Phrygian, on E, and so forth. They were taught the art of descant, by which it was possible to write, and even to improvise in singing, an additional modal melody that would combine harmoniously with a given one. They learned all these rules, not as a dead academic study, but as a method by which they themselves could eventually invent compositions of their own in few or many parts.

Thus they acquired a technic, in the quite ordinary course of their education, which would enable them to express with adequate competence any musical ideas with which they might later find themselves inspired. The laws of harmony they quickly absorbed; ingenuity and expressiveness in the mazes of counter-

---

[32] Morley (1), p. 33. Gaufurius (Franchino Gafori, 1451-1522) was one of the leading theoreticians of his time. See also "A Lesson of Descant of Thirtie-Eighte Proportions of Sundrie Kindes, made by Master Giles, Master of the Children at Windsor," Hawkins, II, 961-963.

[33] *Richard II,* V, v, 41.

point they mastered in time. It is no cause for surprise, then, that a boy like John Milton should have achieved such easy facility as he later displayed, without much additional instruction in later life, nor that so many of his contemporaries should have produced scores which are the marvel and despair of moderns.

When this rather rigorous instruction was concluded for the day, the boys were joined by the eight lay clerks who assumed the alto, tenor, and bass parts in the choir, and a rehearsal of new music was held. A Latin motet was first chosen by Master Blitheman, for Christ Church, as a center of traditional learning, was permitted to preserve the languages of antiquity and some of the ancient forms of liturgical art. This one was a complin, or evening hymn, *Christe qui lux est et dies,* by Robert Whyte, master of the choristers at Westminster Abbey and son-in-law of the famous Doctor Tye.[34] The tenor soloist, accompanied by the organ, delivered the opening phrases. Then the five parts in the chorus were taught to enter successively, in the old polyphonic style, with the words, "Precamur, sancte Domine, defende nos in hac nocte . . ." words which Milton himself was to use for the only motet of his which has been preserved down to the present time. Here, in the rhythmical interweaving of the voices, the choristers had need of all the details of prolation and proportion that they had learned. The harmonies they produced, in the striking Aeolian mode, would sound somewhat weird— almost Oriental—to modern ears.

When this composition was executed to the Master's satisfaction, they turned to a comparatively simple English anthem, "I Give You a New Commandment," by John Shepherd.[35] This composer's name was well known to young Milton and

---

[34] Edited (for modern use) by S. Townsend Warner, *Tudor Church Music,* octavo edition, No. 16, Oxford. See Walker, pp. 34, 42-44.

[35] This composition was printed in Day's *Mornyng and Evenyng Praier.* See also Bumpus, I, 16-17.

his friends and was seldom mentioned without a certain awe.
Shepherd had been "magister choristarum" at Magdalen College and had produced a great quantity of excellent music,
much of which was in the library of Christ Church. He was at
this time chiefly remembered, however, as having been admonished by the authorities for offenses "contra formam statuti."
Finding himself short of good soprano voices, he had gone about
the country and kidnapped and carried into the College some
boys who seemed suitably endowed.

This had been a common practice among the choirmasters of
Henry VIII, and even Elizabeth was not averse to press-gang
methods when sweet-voiced children were scarce in her chapel
at Windsor, Greenwich, or Whitehall. Impressed choir boys
were often treated rather brutally—at least so the rumors ran—
since care had to be taken to prevent them from running away.[36]
Shepherd's offense was not that he had simply entrapped a few
"meet and apt" boys with "good breasts" nor that he had mis-
treated his captives, but that he had done so without a Royal
license. The Christ Church choristers might well indulge in a
few dramatic and not altogether unpleasant shudders at the
possibility, vague as it was, of being snatched off to the Queen's
establishment some day.

Master Blitheman next brought out *The Actes of the
Apostles*, by the celebrated Dr. Christopher Tye,[37] printed in
1553, "very necessary for students after their study, to file their
wits, and also for all Christians that cannot sing to read the good
and Godly stories of the lives of Christ and his apostles." Tye
had been music master to Edward VI, to whom the work was

---

[36] *Ibid.*, I, 25-26, 102-103.

[37] See Hawkins, I, 452-454; Burney, III, 10-11; Nagel, II, pp. 59-61; Bumpus,
I, 30-35. At present there is no modern edition of the *Actes* in print with the
original words. Novello, however, publishes most of them separately, with different anthem-texts; e.g., *Short Anthems*, Nos. 115, 215, 163, 137, 212 (chap.
ix, the simple canon), 135, 213 (chap. xiv, the double canon).

dedicated, and had continued to serve royalty in his profession. The *Actes* were simple but artful settings, in four parts, of metrical summaries of the first fourteen chapters of that book. The verses, concocted by the composer himself, were almost a *reductio ad absurdum* of the method then fashionable among the Puritans of turning Holy Writ, particularly the psalms, into doggerel—a method with which the Miltons, both father and son, were later to have much to do. The music was far sounder and more ingenious than the words. Master Blitheman required his choristers to sing the tabloid version of Chapter IX:

> Saul, breathing out threatnings abroad,
> The faithful to resist,
> Against the 'lect of God the Lord,
> Went unto the high priest. . . .

Here the treble and alto voices sang in strict canon, the altos leading off and the sopranos following, note for note and a fourth above. The Master called the attention to this device, the strictest form of musical imitation. Then, after a few more chapters, in simpler style, had been sung, he turned to the fourteenth:

> It chanced in Iconium,
> As they did ofttimes use,
> Together they unto did come
> The synagogue of Jews. . . .

For this literary hideosity, Dr. Tye had achieved, strangely enough, a genuinely inspired musical *tour de force,* a strict canon "four in two." While the trebles followed the altos at a distance of a fourth, the tenors followed the basses at a distance of a sixth. The whole composition contained only three noncanonical notes, at the very close. And yet the thing was carried out with the greatest melodic smoothness and apparent spontaneity—which, as Blitheman remarked, distinguished this tiny masterpiece from hundreds of canons by lesser men; canons which, although they displayed far more colossal erudition (turning the subject upside down, reading it backward, and torturing it in many more ingenious and fiendish ways), failed to disclose anything more than vast academic aridity.

The master had reserved his pleasantest item for the very end of the day's instruction. He announced that the choristers were soon to begin rehearsing a play, which would be ready for performance during the coming Christmas season. This statement immediately excited everbody. Plays were tremendous fun and were gladly supported by financial grants from the House authorities. Some radical reformers, indeed, condemned them as a satanic and lascivious art, but it was well known that the Virgin Queen herself delighted in them. One Master Richard Edwards,[38] who had died only a few years before, had done more than any other man to establish a strong dramatic tradition both at the Royal Court and at Christ Church. He had been one of the very first students in the House, at the time of its foundation in 1547. He had composed the first really successful English madrigal, "In Going to My Naked Bed";[39] he had composed verses in Hebrew, Greek, Latin, and English, and had sung them to the lute before his pupils;[40] he had been master of the boys at the Chapel Royal; his plays for boy actors had delighted the Queen, one of them, *Palaemon and Arcyte,* having been presented before her here at Christ Church on her first visit to Oxford, in 1566. So now young Milton and his friends knew that there was at least a possibility that Elizabeth herself might hear them act and sing. One never could predict just when a place would be suddenly honored by a royal visitation; and, failing the presence of Majesty, there would always be an

[38] Flood, pp. 112-115.
[39] Definitively edited by E. H. Fellowes in Vol. XXXVI of *The English Madrigal School.* Most of the earlier editions are faulty, some going so far in prudery as to change "naked" in the title to "lonely."
[40] Nagel, II, 51-52.

audience of great nobility, or artistic eminence, or ecclesiastical dignity.

The play for this season, Master Blitheman explained, would present the very sorrowful story of Panthea and Abradates. It would contain many songs, and its climax was to be marked by the heroine's most grievous lament for the death of her husband. One of Milton's companions, a pretty, slender boy with a sweet treble voice, was assigned to the enviable role of Panthea. The dirge which he was to sing was to be accompanied by four other choristers playing on viols. For this item, Master Richard Farrant, also a famous choirmaster, had written the music, and it was now given a brief preliminary rehearsal.

Above the grave tones of the strings the boy began singing "Alas, ye salt sea gods . . ." and he waxed right doleful as he familiarized himself with the tune: "Abradad, Abradad, ah, ah, alas, poor Abradad!"—in the manner which Shakespeare was later to satirize so hilariously in the burlesque play of Pyramus and Thisbe in *A Midsummer Night's Dream*.[41] But on this day even this rather halting performance was hugely enjoyed, everyone offering whatever suggestions he could as to the probable behavior of an exquisitely bereaved lady. The boys were then released for a brief period of recreation and private study.

Most of them took a natural delight in bodily exercise, physical fitness having been recognized by their more progressive masters as desirable even in scholars and musicians. They competed with one another in running, leaping, pitching the bar, tennis, bowling, fighting with the singlestick, wrestling (with benefit of very few rules of politeness or safety), and in a very rough and haphazard melee called "football." Inveterate young intellectuals, however, preferred to remain indoors and play at chess or draughts—or even to pore over Lilly's Latin grammar or to write a few counterpoint exercises.

[41] *The Musical Antiquary*, October, 1909, pp. 30-40; January, 1913, pp. 112-117. See also Warlock (1), p. 128.

So the time was passed until the hour of Evening Prayer, when all again repaired to the chapel. At this service the music was simpler than in the morning, the usual responses being sung in unison to John Marbeck's *Book of Common Prayer Noted*,[42] the earliest and most famous adaptation of the simple medieval plain chant to the English reformed rite. The required canticles, the Magnificat and Nunc Dimittis, were taken from Tallis's plain and severe music in the Dorian mode.[43] In this work the composer had eschewed all learned and fanciful elaboration and had for once adhered scrupulously to the requirements of the Protestant leaders. It contained no canonic or imitative devices, and no deftly interwoven polyphony, but moved in solid blocks of harmony, with a note to each syllable of the text. The effect was that of a kind of musical granite, massive and imposing in its own ponderous way.

But although the radical reformers hoped that such weighty homeliness would eventually drive out all the color and ornament of the older style, very few musicians were pessimistic enough to agree with them. Master Tallis himself, although he had produced this Dorian Service as part of his official activity, had thrown his main energy into his Latin polyphonic compositions, which could be sung at the universities or as vocal chamber music in the private establishments of the very rich. English church music was flourishing too vigorously to be stunted by the restrictions that had been aimed at its natural growth.

So much, at any rate, was sufficiently apparent to the Christ Church musicians, old and young. For they themselves were both producing and rendering music, sacred and secular, in many widely different styles. And simply because no single style had been completely accepted as a stereotyped standard, they felt quite free to experiment, to absorb, and to develop to the full all the inspirations, ideas, and varieties of technique they knew.

[42] Bumpus, I, 5-9, 12-13.   [43] Printed complete in Boyce, I, 1-43.

They may have been at least vaguely conscious of the fact that they were even then standing at the very threshold of what was to be the most glorious and exciting era in the history of English music.

And so, looking forward with some ardor to the morrow's music and to what the coming months and years would bring, young Milton proceeded to his ample supper of meat and bread. Soon night began to fall over the halls and streets of the ancient town. A few tallow candles were lighted in the Hall; amiable and desultory conversation was carried on by the masters and the pupils. But not for long—the illumination, although rather expensive, was not of good quality, and presently the lights were being extinguished.

Milton made his way up a narrow stairway, found his simple pallet, removed his outer clothing, and washed sketchily. Then he knelt and prayed, repeating the words of his favorite motet: "... sit nobis in te requies; quietam noctem tribue. Deo Patri sit gloria, eiusque soli Filio, cum Spiritu paracleto, et nunc et in perpetuum, Amen." And he was safely and dutifully asleep long before Great Tom tolled the hour of nine.

CHAPTER II

Oxford and the Polish Prince

1573-1585

THE YOUNG John Milton probably spent many hundreds of days such as the one which has just been described. At least four of the most impressionable years of his boyhood, following 1573, were given over to his training as an Oxford chorister.[1] These years sufficed to saturate him with elementary classical learning and with the most eloquent music of his time. Next to the Chapel Royal itself, there was in the whole Kingdom no establishment with a more vigorously maintained musical tradition than Christ Church. A brief account of this tradition may help to illuminate the story of Milton's cultural development.

The institution had been founded in 1525 as Cardinal's College; it was one of the grandiose cultural projects of the mighty Wolsey. With its annual revenues of £2,000, it had at first supported a dean and a hundred canons. For its daily hours of prayer it had maintained a staff of thirteen chaplains, twelve lay clerks, sixteen choristers, and a teacher of music. The last had been John Taverner, the greatest of English pre-Reformation musicians.[2] His official title was "informator" of the children;

---

[1] It has been suggested, probably with little justification, that Milton may also have been resident at Magdalen College at some time. If it is true, then he would have been under the rule of Lawrence Humphrey, President of Magdalen, an extreme Puritan; and one of his schoolfellows would have been Father Anthony Greenway (alias Tilney, S. J.), who was at Magdalen from his eleventh to his twentieth year and was converted to the Roman faith at twenty-one. See Henry Foley, S. J.: *Records of the English Province of the Society of Jesus*, first series, London, Burns and Oates, 1877, I, 466-468.

[2] The bulk of Taverner's extant music, superbly edited, together with much

25

his salary and allowances had amounted to £15 per year, an honorarium exceeded only by those of the dean and the sub-dean. One Anthony Delaber, in telling the story of a heretic hunt which took place around 1530, describes a scene in the chapel: "Evensong was begun, and the Dean and the other canons were there in their grey amices; they were almost at *Magnificat* before I came thither. I stood at the choir door and heard Master Taverner play, and others of the chapel there sing." [3] He goes on, rather pathetically, to tell how the music, usually so joyously delivered, was on this occasion clouded over with the apprehension that accompanied the religious troubles of the time.

Cardinal's College had been ruthlessly suppressed by King Henry, but was re-established in 1546 as Christ Church. St. Frideswide's then became not only the chapel of the college but also the cathedral church of the diocese. This new Foundation, with an income of £2,200 per annum, was managed by a corporation consisting of a dean and eight canons. It supported three "public professors," in theology, Hebrew, and Greek, a hundred students,[4] eight chaplains, eight lay clerks, eight *pueri musici*, as well as sacristans, porters, and other servants.[5]

John Piers, who had been dean since 1570, was succeeded in 1576 by Tobie Matthews, a good scholar and theologian, who nevertheless won a reputation as a liberal; under him the fine arts, including music, undoubtedly received plenty of encouragement. Assuming his exalted office at the tender age of thirty, he managed to combine severe learning with amiability and wit.

---

biographical and critical material, has been reprinted in Vols. I and III of *Tudor Church Music.*

[3] The account is quoted in Fox's *Acts and Monuments*, ed. 1583, II, 1195.

[4] The position of Student at Christ Church apparently corresponded roughly with that of Fellow in the other Oxford Colleges.

[5] Thompson, pp. 12, 34, 36. In the official accounts no mention is made of the post of Master of the Choristers, the position which Blitheman occupied in Milton's time. But there can be no doubt that the office existed.

He was accustomed to say that he "could as well not be, as not be merry." [6] With such a man dictating the policies of the College and responsible only to the Queen, the students and choristers must have enjoyed an unusual amount of personal liberty. Milton was subject only to such reasonable repressions as the quaintly phrased chapter order requiring that "no student, scholar, chaplain, nor servant or any belonging to the House shall lodge any dog except the porter to drive out cattle and hogs out of the house." But he was prohibited from indulging any inclination toward frippery in his costume: "Scholars shall not wear any white and pricked doublets, no galligaskins or cut hose, no welted or laced gowns, upon the several pains next before rehearsed." [7]

It appears that the College was at this time open to some students not provided for by the Foundation. Their names were never entered in the books, but they were nevertheless under tuition there. Such non-foundationers were lodged nearby in Broadgates Hall. Among them were William Camden, later the famous antiquary and historian, who became a pupil of one of the canons, Dr. Thomas Thornton. Another was Philip Sidney, likewise a protege of Thornton and destined to become the paragon of his age. He had come to Oxford at the age of fourteen, and although he left in 1571 on account of the plague then raging, he may have associated with or even befriended Milton, who was his junior by eight years.

With somewhat greater certainty one can say that Milton must have met and known, more or less intimately, Richard Hakluyt, who was elected a student from Westminster in 1570; William Gager, the classical dramatist, who resided there many years on his studentship; and George Peele, who had come from Christ's Hospital and had entered Broadgates Hall before being appointed a student. Gager and Peele were naturally in-

[6] Thompson, pp. 30-31.   [7] *Ibid.*, pp. 39-41.

terested chiefly in the stage, and Christ Church gave them splendid opportunities to exercise their dramatic talents.

Ever since the Queen's visit in 1566, when she had been lodged at Christ Church (the dean and canons gladly vacating their chambers to provide accommodations for the royal person and retinue), the drama had flourished in the House. For "the pastime in Christmas and the plays" the authorities allowed to be expended the sum of £6; of this sum twenty shillings were allotted to a Greek comedy, twenty to a Latin comedy, and forty each to a Greek and Latin tragedy.[8] For plays in the vernacular there was no subvention, but lack of funds did not prevent their production.

For all these, incidental music was required, and the resources of the chapel provided both voices and instruments. Stage directions called for "consorts" of recorders or pipes, to be used in pastoral scenes or to heighten the effect of dolorous dialogue, hautboys for moments of greater stress, trumpets to punctuate martial declamation, viols for amatory passages. Regals or small organs were also used for mournful scenes. For the dumb shows, "broken consorts" were used, consisting of several different kinds of instruments, including plucked and stroked strings, wind, brass, and drums, playing together. And of course there were the solo airs, sung to the lute or regal, and choruses.[9]

Although secular and instrumental music was at this time rather simple as compared to the elaboration that characterized the religious vocal polyphony, the choir boys of Christ Church did not lack opportunities for practice in the fields that lay outside their ecclesiastical duties. Certainly Milton, as a member of

[8] *Ibid.*, p. 50.

[9] This very rough summary of dramatic music is based on what we know of the production of such plays as Legge's *Richardus Tertius* (see Smith, pp. 9, 46, Howes, pp. 190-193; Chambers, III, 407-408), Edwards's *Damon and Pythias*, Gascoigne's *Jocasta*, and Munday's *The Two Italian Gentlemen*. For a somewhat more detailed account of the subject, see Cowling, pp. 14-21.

what amounted to a choir school, received musical training and experience such as was denied to the older and regular pupils and students of the House. For there was not yet anything approaching musical education in the college itself. The first music lecture at Oxford was not founded until 1626.[10]

On the more firmly established field of liturgic and devotional music, the conflict between old and new was still being carried on. In this conflict the issues were both religious and esthetic, and were destined to have complicated and interesting results. There was first the tendency to retain the traditional language and ceremonial apparatus of the Church of Rome, which was encouraged both by the High Church party and by musicians who were loath to discard the highly developed technique that they had mastered and loved. Opposed to them were the reformers who insisted on the use of the vernacular and on extreme simplification.

To summarize the outcome briefly, one may say that both sides won partial victories. Elizabeth herself had used characteristic caution at first. She had been crowned according to the ceremonies of the Roman pontifical, and she offended some bishops by allowing in her private chapel "the cross on the altar, and two candelsticks and two tapers burning." But she consented to the use of the English litany, which had been prepared by Cranmer in 1544. And presently the English service as set forth in the *Revised Prayer Book* of Edward VI was ordered for all churches. Thus the English canticles and the anthem drove out the Latin mass and the motet, the latter being relegated to more or less surreptitious private devotions and to certain favored university chapels.

The movement to simplify the music, however, did not in the end succeed. Ingenious composers and well-trained choirs made only half-hearted attempts to adhere strictly to the principle of

[10] Hawkins, I, 465.

"a modest and distinct song," as we have seen, and it was not long before such comparatively unadorned services as those of Causton and Tallis gave way to the larger polyphonic designs which were best represented by the "great" Service of William Byrd. And the anthems became as elaborate as the older motets had ever been.[11]

It was only in the increasing popularity of the metrical psalms, very plainly harmonized, that the puritans won any considerable victory. The custom of singing rhymed versions of the psalter had originated among the Calvinists at Geneva and had spread rapidly over the whole of Protestant Europe. It apparently represented the only species of devotional music that was endurable to the consciences of the more extreme reformers. In England, Wyatt, Surrey, and Coverdale had been the first to produce metrical psalms, but the version that took the swiftest and most permanent hold, in spite of its being largely doggeral verse of small literary merit, was the one started by Sternhold in 1549 and later completed by Hopkins and others. For this text, music was supplied in a series of publications ranging from 1553 to the eighteenth century. In quality these settings varied greatly, from the fantastically clumsy to the purest in melody and harmony. Almost every composer of any pretentions whatsoever made his contribution to them at some time or other.[12] For many generations Milton the composer was remembered only as a psalmodist.

Metrical psalms were used chiefly for private recreation and devotion, and their employment was by no means restricted to puritan households. In an age when the secular art song had scarcely been born and before even the madrigal, a more difficult species of composition to perform, had attained any great vogue,

---

[11] See the "Historical Survey" in *Tudor Church Music*, I, xvi-xxxiii; also Fellows (3), pp. 9-12.

[12] A full survey of the subject is to be found in Wooldridge (2). See also pp. 98-101.

it was inevitable that the psalms, which could easily be sung with excellent harmonic effects by four or more voices, should satisfy a genuine need for musical expression among all classes of persons. There is little justification for assuming that they were not enthusiastically sung at Oxford, as everywhere else, and by both Falstaffs and Philip Sidneys.[13]

Furthermore, they were quickly admitted into the regular services of the Church, not indeed as a substitute for the prescribed canticles, but in addition to them. This was specifically allowed in the Elizabethan Injunctions of 1559: "that in the beginning or in the end of Common Prayers, either at morning or evening, there may be sung an hymn, or such like song to the praise of Almighty God, in the best sort of music that may be conveniently devised, having respect that the sentence of the hymn may be understood and perceived." Thus we find often repeated on the title pages of early psalters the notation that they are "set forth and allowed to be sung in all churches of all the people together, before and after Morning and Evening Prayer, and also before and after Sermons; and moreover in private houses, for their godly solace and comfort." [14]

Two musical events occurred in 1575, while Milton was still singing treble parts in the Christ Church choir, and they are of some significance for the understanding of his early artistic environment. The first was the monopoly granted by the Queen to her "well beloved servants Thomas Tallis and William Byrd"

---

[13] "I would I were a weaver; I could sing psalms or anything," cries the Fat Knight (*1. Henry IV*, II, iv, 137); the passage is explained by the fact that psalmody was especially popular among the woollen manufacturers, mostly Flemish Protestants who had taken refuge in England. Falstaff also says, "For my voice, I have lost it with hollaing, and singing of anthems." (*2. Henry IV*, I, ii, 182) Sidney's enthusiasm for even more popular music than the psalms (e.g., the ballads) is well known.

[14] Procter, pp. 174-177. When the new order of Morning Prayer was inaugurated at St. Antholin's in London, "a Psalm was sung after the Geneva fashion, all the congregation, men, women and boys, singing together." Procter, p. 59.

for the printing and selling of all music and music paper.[15] Tallis was at this time seventy years of age, Byrd only thirty-two; both were organists of the Royal Chapel. The second event was the joint publication by the same two composers of their *Cantiones quae ab argumento sacrae vocantur*, a set of motets for five and six voices, of which sixteen were by Tallis and eighteen by Byrd. These compositions represented the older man's supreme achievement, with the possible exception of his forty-voiced motet, *Spem in alium*. And Byrd's share in both events—his endorsement by the older school, and his striking new contributions—mark his definite ascendancy to the leadership in English music, which he was to retain for the remaining years of the century. So well did he acquit himself during those years that today, in the opinion of the most competent critics, he disputes only with Purcell the position of England's greatest composer.

Since John Milton as a musician belonged definitely to the school of Byrd, although twenty years his junior, an idea of Byrd's accomplishment provides an excellent foundation for a just view of the younger man's activity. Byrd's work was,[16] to begin with, firmly grounded on the older ecclesiastical methods. In the composition of masses and motets he demonstrated that he had fully absorbed all that Tallis had achieved. He continued to write Latin church music throughout his long life, even

---

[15] The document is printed in Fellowes (3), pp. 7-8. Elizabeth made the grant "for the special affection and good will that we have and bear to the science of music and for the advancement thereof." This phraseology need not be entirely discounted as a conventional formula, since the Queen's intensely personal interest in music has been well established.

[16] Fellowes (3) and Howes supply excellent monographs on Byrd. His masses, motets, services, and anthems will be found in Vols. II, VII, and IX of *Tudor Church Music;* his madrigals and a few solo songs and fantasias for strings in *English Madrigal School*, Vols. XIV, XV, and XVI; his keyboard music in the *Fitzwilliam Virginal Book, Lady Nevell's Book,* and *Parthenia*. Many reprints of separate compositions, as well as gramophone records, are available. A definitive edition of his vocal works is at present (1938) being edited by Fellowes for Stainer and Bell.

though such music could receive no public performance. This is partially explained by the facts that he remained a Roman Catholic and that his deepest sympathies undoubtedly lay in the ancient traditions. At the same time he served Elizabeth well, enjoyed her personal protection, and wrote voluminously for the English rite.

Historically, however, his importance lies largely in his more experimental work. In his *Turbarum voces* [17] he set for a three-part chorus the responses of the people in the Passion according to St. John, anticipating the dramatic oratorios of the seventeenth and eighteenth centuries. He was the first English composer to develop with complete success the polyphonic secular madrigal. He was the first to produce meritorious keyboard music in any considerable quantity. His attempts at solo songs with accompaniments for strings and his fantasias for viols did not reach extraordinary merit, but in these untried fields he was a path breaker. In his pioneer endeavors the younger men of his time found invaluable guidance, and his influence could not fail to reach and impress the young Milton.

Milton could not have sung soprano parts long after the year 1577, for at that time his voice must have broken, and some consequent change in his status at Christ Church must have taken place. For the year 1577, too, we have an item of information which shows that his father had then achieved the rating of a man of considerable substance. The parish records of Stanton St. John indicate that in that year the goods of Richard Milton were assessed at the respectable sum of £5 for a subsidy. From this we may safely conclude that Richard had now become one of the most prosperous citizens of his station in his own community.

What happened to John Milton after 1577? He must have

[17] *Tudor Church Music*, VII, 202-205. A modern reprint, with English translation, has been published by Novello.

visited his parents frequently, but he probably remained under instruction at Christ Church. Several opportunities were open to him, as a promising youth of good substantial family, and with the beginnings of a satisfactory classical and musical education. He could at the very least have qualified for the not very exalted ranks of the *pauperes scholares,* as the servitor or attendant on a richer undergraduate. If he did, he was paid two shillings and fourpence per week for his maintenance, his food consisting of what was left when his master's meals were over. Only four servitors were allowed at the High Table; they were required to "go in gowns always, and to lie within the precincts of the Church." They attended public prayers, of course, and also "the exercises of lectures and disputations according to their standings." [18]

Or with better luck he could have made his way into the student body, as a nonfoundationer or an undercommoner. But it is most probable that, when his voice had completely changed to bass or tenor, he continued as a singing man or lay clerk in the chapel. In one capacity or another he remained there, becoming at least a moderately skilled Latinist, so that many years later his son could address to him, without any incongruity, the lengthy and neoclassical epistle *Ad Patrem.* That his university career lasted six years more, until 1583, seems to be demonstrated by an entertaining event which must now be recorded.

A certain Polish prince, wrote the biographer Edward Phillips, rewarded John Milton the elder with a gold chain and medal for composing an *In Nomine* of forty parts. For this statement Phillips gave the word of Milton the poet as his authority, and we have therefore little reason to suspect its reliability. [19] Now the only Polish dignitary who is known to have

---

[18] Thompson, pp. 58-59.

[19] Aubrey (Milton [3] p. xxii) makes a similar statement about a "song of four score parts" written for the Landgrave of Hesse, a statement which may represent a less accurate version of Phillips's account. This possibility is discussed more fully in chap. iv, pp. 66-68.

visited England at this period was one Albertus Alasco, free baron of Lasco, vaiode, or count palatine, of Siradia, a duchy in Lower Poland, where he is said to have owned no less than fifty castles. This magnate not only made a visit of state to the royal Court at London but also journeyed to Oxford and was lodged at Christ Church. He apparently had no specific diplomatic mission, but acted as a kind of informal ambassador of good will, a role for which he was eminently qualified, as will appear. His visit took place in 1583, during Milton's twentieth year, the last year that he spent at Oxford. Contemporary annalists have described the circumstances with a remarkable wealth of detail.[20]

Alasco arrived at Harwich in April and proceeded immediately to London, where he took up his residence at Winchester House, in Southwark. At his first opportunity he paid his formal respects to the Queen. Anthony Wood describes him as follows: "of an indifferent tall stature, of countenance amiable, and complexion English-like, having a white beard of such length and breadth, as that lying in his bed and parting it with his hands, the same overspread all his breast and shoulders, himself greatly delighting therein, and reputing it an ornament." Other eyewitnesses testify to the magnificence of this beard. Camden mentions it somewhat dryly but goes on to characterize the Count as "a man most learned, of comely stature and lineaments, richly clothed and of graceful behavior." We learn further from Wood that he was "generous"—excessively so, as we shall see—"his utterance sweet, his wit plausible; his ordinary attire scarlet, but when he presented himself to her Majesty, a robe or gown of purple velvet. His shoes of a strange fashion, supposed of some not altogether unlike Chaucer's. A gallant fellow, more martial than mercurial, very active in respect to his age, and also studious in diverse faculties."

[20] The chief sources of information for the account which follows are Rye, p. iv, who quotes Camden's *Annales*, London, 1625, Book 3, p. 42; and Nichols, II, 398, 405-410, who quotes Anthony Wood and Holinshed, 25. *Elizabeth*.

This superb showman soon enchanted the royal court, with its notorious enthusiasm for the spectacular and the exotic. "The Queen with much bounty and love received him," wrote Camden; "the nobles with great honor and magnificence entertained him," little suspecting that possibly he was just a trifle too gaudy to be altogether reliable. After his beard, his quaint attire, and his plausible wit (Elizabeth herself must have bandied elegant repartee with him in Latin) had cast their spell over the brilliant society at the capital, he went on to Oxford to be delighted with more learned recreations.

For many days the university had been preparing for his visitation, sparing no trouble, ingenuity, or expense. Tobie Matthews, the jolly young dean, could not resist this opportunity to engineer a gigantic display for the colorful and charming man of the world. Alasco, with his retinue, arrived at Oxford in June. As he approached the East Gate, he discovered the mayor, aldermen, and bailiffs of the city, in their scarlet, drawn up to receive him. Dr. Westfailing delivered to him a "pithy salutation" in behalf of the university; the mayor came forward with a sententious speech in Latin and presented him with a pair of gloves as a gift from the corporation.

Over the gate stood a consort of musicians, equipped with wind instruments, and at this moment they began playing. They made very sweet harmony, which, according to Holinshed, "could not but move and delight." The music continued thus for a long time, until the whole procession had moved slowly through the gate and into the city. On both sides of High Street were marshalled the university scholars in gowns and caps and the bachelors and masters in their habits and hoods. The parade moved up to St. Mary's Church, where the orator of the university presented Alasco with a book. On opening it, the prince was doubtless thrilled to perceive, closely folded in its pages, another pair of very rich and gorgeous gloves. Thence to Christ

Church, where he was to sup and lodge in comfort every night.

His first evening was given over to rest and refreshment, his entertainers mercifully deciding that he had better be fortified for the diversions to come. Consequently, after supper he did nothing but watch a display of strange fireworks, including rockets, in the great quadrangle. The next morning he was claimed by All Souls College. There he attended divine service, at which the Latin office was probably sung in his honor, featuring a mass and motets by English composers, and he listened patiently to a Latin sermon. After dinner he viewed several copies of verses composed by members of the college, curiously painted with colors and hung up on the walls. That night he repaired to the Hall of Christ Church with his entire train for a performance of *Rivales*, a frivolous Latin comedy by Dr. Gager, which was staged by George Peele.

On the third day he listened to Latin disputations, debates being then as now a favorite species of academic entertainment. The propositions on this occasion were two: *An sit divinatio per stellas?* and *An mares vivant diutius quam feminae?* Such questions having been settled, presumably to everyone's satisfaction, Alasco attended another Latin play by Gager, the stately tragedy of *Dido*. This time Peele outdid himself in the staging, especially in the scene of the Queen's banquet, in which Aeneas delivered his bombastic narrative of the destruction of Troy. This episode, wrote Holinshed, "was lively described in a marchpaine pattern; there was also a goodly sight of hunters with full cry of a kennel of hounds, Mercury and Iris descending and ascending from and to an high place, the tempest wherein it hailed small confects, rained rose water, and snew an artificial kind of snow, all strange, marvelous, and abundant." At the conclusion of this spectacle, Gager had the honor to receive from the Prince his personal thanks.

There were of course many more orations, presentations,

feasts, disputations and diversions, but, as Holinshed remarks, enough has been set forth to suffice "for a sudden remembrance." When the time for departure came, the procession moved out of the town by the North Gate and proceeded to St. John's College for a final banquet, where the gates and outer walls were covered with thousands of verses of good will—St. John's having doggedly resolved to outdo All Souls once and for all. But the exhausted Count was not yet through with scholarly pastimes. For the first two miles of his journey back to London he was accompanied by the doctors and heads of Houses on horseback and in their scarlet gowns—then a pause and ultimate leavetaking by the roadside, where the university orator delivered the final farewell.

Once safely back in London, Alasco gave to the Queen such a glowing report on his treatment that the university presently received a special note of thanks from the royal hand. This appreciation was richly deserved, for the colleges had expended no less than £350 on the festivities. Of this sum Peele received £18 for his services in mounting and directing the two plays. Never before had the university carried off so magnificent a display for a noble of Alasco's degree.

But the authorities at Oxford, as well as the royal court, probably felt some mortification when the closing episode of the Prince's visit transpired. He had responded to the English hospitality with an appropriately lavish hand, distributing rich awards—and making purchases for which local merchants were flattered to extend credit. Thus he spent four extravagant months in the country. He departed on the twenty-first of September, but without any pomp or display whatsoever. As Camden laconically puts it, "Finding himself overcharged with debt, he privily stole away." He was forced to flee thus from his anxious creditors, notwithstanding that he was possessed of fifty Polish castles which, as Holinshed gloomily remarked, were "of great value,—with a wife." An English gentleman, Sir Richard Baker, later caught a glimpse of him at Cracow, "very poor and bare."

We have described this visit rather fully, not only because it makes a diverting story but chiefly because of Milton's share in the festivities. Literary and musical critics have sometimes felt inclined to doubt the whole story of the *In Nomine* of forty parts and the gold chain and medal, chiefly on the assumption that a composition of forty real parts (that is, with forty voices or instruments performing independently at the same time) is an almost incredible feat for an amateur composer. Furthermore, with the exception of the consort over the East Gate, no mention of music for Alasco was made by Holinshed, Camden, or Aubrey. But there must have been much singing and fiddling, at the banquets, receptions, plays, and church services. And the circumstances we know make Phillips's statement extremely plausible.

In the first place, a tremendously complicated musical work, displaying enormous technical ingenuity, would have been considered eminently fitting, by way of impressing the distinguished Eastern visitor; it would go well with the fireworks, the learned disputations, the thousands of commendatory Latin verses. Further, it is just the sort of academic extravagance that would have tempted a musically inclined youth of twenty. Again, compositions in forty real parts were by no means unheard of at this period. A story is told about John Bull, Milton's exact contemporary, in which he is represented as traveling incognito on the Continent and being shown a composition in forty parts; whereupon he demanded paper and pen of its composer, and immediately added another forty to it—and the composer, overcome with admiration at this diabolical feat, fell down on his knees and worshipped him.[21]

---

[21] The story is told in Hawkins, I, 480. Probably it has only a very meager foundation in fact, not because Bull's feat might be considered incredible, but, on the contrary, because continental composers had for years been accustomed to amuse themselves with similar stunts.

That story may be apocryphal, but there is no doubt whatever that another English master, Thomas Tallis himself, did produce a forty-part motet, the score of which is still extant and has been published.[22] This composition, to the words *Spem in alium nunquam habui*, is laid out for eight five-part choirs. The remarkable thing about it is that it is not only a colossal technical *tour de force* but also an inspiring piece of music.[23] Even Dr. Burney, who had little sympathy for any of the music of this time, describes it in the following Johnsonian verbiage: "This stupendous, though perhaps Gothic, specimen of human labor and intellect, is carried on in alternate flight, pursuit, attack, and choral union to the end; when the Polyphonic Phenomenon is terminated by twelve bars of universal chorus, in quadragintesimal harmony."[24] The work has enjoyed a number of performances during the last century, by the Henry Leslie Choir (expanded to 240 singers for the occasion), by Dr. A. H. Mann's choir at London, by the Newcastle-upon-Tyne Choir, and by the Chicago A Cappella Choir.[25]

Another reason why Milton probably was delighted to produce a big *In Nomine* for Alasco is that the *In Nomine* was a distinctively English form, based on a certain plainsong melody, and unknown on the Continent. By doing so he seized another chance to enrapture the visiting foreigners with a taste of his own national art. A final shred of argument is the fact that Milton produced other *In Nomines*, one of which, written for only six parts, has survived and will be analyzed later.[26] The Alasco composition may have been for voices alone, or for voices and instruments, or for instruments alone. If the last, then it is barely possible that it was played by the consort over the East Gate,

[22] *Tudor Church Music*, VI, xxxiii, xli, 299-318.
[23] See Walker, pp. 45-46.   [24] Burney, III, 74-75.
[25] See Davey, p. 135; also *Choral Music and Its Practice*, by Noble Cain, New York, Witmark, 1932, pp. 114-118.
[26] See pp. 139-142.

which in that case consisted of no less than forty performers of cornets, sackbuts, and recorders. Of course it may not have been performed at all; but at any rate the Count rewarded the proud musician when he perused the incredible score, doubtless in an impressive ceremony. We are not told what eventually became of the gold medal and chain. Milton may have been forced to return it to one of Alasco's disgruntled creditors.

This was the high spot in Milton's university career, which must have come to a sudden and dramatic close shortly afterward, because of a domestic crisis at Stanton St. John. Richard Milton had been elected a churchwarden of the parish in 1582, the year before Alasco's visit. This honor should have gratified him immensely, as another definite step forward in his career. But it was probably a highly embarrassing event for the good yeoman and father. For it happened, ironically enough, at just about the time that he apparently became converted to the Roman Catholic Church.

That he permitted himself to be swept out of the Anglican Communion at this date, and to risk the serious disabilities to which papists were subjected under Elizabeth, argues that he must have passed through an intellectual and emotional crisis of some intensity. Subsequent events were to prove that the ardor and firmness that one expects from a convert were not lacking in his mind. But precisely how he reconciled his new religious fervor with his churchwarden's duties of managing the local Church of England property and seeing that proper precedence was observed in seating the parishoners at the services, we have no means of ascertaining. Possibly some of his neighbors, suspecting his leanings toward Rome, had contrived the election in a friendly but vain attempt to bring the man to his senses. Possibly, being jealous of his worldly success, they had done it maliciously, in order to visit acute embarrassment upon him. He may have kept his conversion secret for a time and welcomed the election as a cloak for his Romish activities. If so, the secret was badly kept. Not long afterward the damning notation *cot* (standing for *contumax*) was written after his name in the record of the arch-deacon's visitation of the parish. He had stubbornly and contumaciously refused to attend Divine Service and had laid himself open to definite penalties. Catholic recusants not only were looked upon as religious backsliders; they also were suspected of political treason, a most serious matter.

He continued to prosper, however, in spite of his voluntary disgrace. In July of 1601 he was fined the enormous sum of £60 for three months' nonattendance, and again £60 for the same offense later in the year. It is quite possible that the loss of £120, equivalent to at least £800 in modern money, and the likelihood of losing all his hard-won wealth for the sake of his convictions, broke him completely. But this must remain a mystery to us. With the opening of the seventeenth century he vanishes forever from the picture, for we know nothing more about his career, excepting the interesting item of his final relations with his son.

One of Richard's earliest acts upon becoming an open recusant was probably to remove John from Christ Church, since he could scarcely tolerate his son's continuance in the contaminating environment of a heretical university and cathedral. It would be vastly interesting to have some clue as to the nature of the conversations between father and son after John's return to the parental roof. But all we know is the climax of the story. One day Richard discovered an English Bible in John's chamber. He acted promptly on this horrifying discovery. He disinherited his son.[27]

[27] The account here given of Richard's recusancy and John's disinheritance seems to harmonize most readily with all ascertainable facts and with the slightly confused stories told by Aubrey and Phillips. Masson (Vol. I, chap. i), with some other commentators, regards it as possible that Richard had always been a Roman

John might indeed have forestalled this misfortune by bowing a submissive knee to his father, pleading for a reconciliation, and accepting the Roman faith. We know from later events in his life that his manners were usually mild and that he had a remarkably sympathetic and conciliatory mind. But in a matter of such ultimate importance as this he displayed a laudable firmness. He adhered to his Anglican convictions and left his father's house, never to return.[28]

There was only one place for an eager young man to go—to the great, glittering, sordid city wherein the nobles, adventurers, statesmen, and wits of the whole Kingdom were now gathering to hasten the progress of the English Renaissance. By 1585, at about the same time that his contemporary, Shakespeare, came from Stratford to the capital, John Milton was also on his way to London to seek his fortune.

Catholic, or had been converted to Rome long before 1582, that John had been brought up in the Roman faith and was disinherited for turning to Anglicanism around his twentieth year. But great difficulties prevent an acceptance of this theory. Richard, as a papist, would scarcely have sent his son to Anglican Oxford; an Oxford college would scarcely have accepted a Romish boy as a chorister; Richard, if a bigoted Catholic of many years' standing, could scarcely have been elected churchwarden. Finally, there is no evidence whatever of Richard's Catholicism before 1582.

[28] See Phillips's account, in Milton (3), p. xxxii; also Wood, p. xxvi; Aubrey, p. xxii; the anonymous biographer, p. xvi.

CHAPTER III

London and Oriana

1585-1603

MILTON, a youth of twenty-two, was literally swallowed up by the teeming city. For a whole decade he managed somehow to live there without leaving any surviving record of his activities. This was a not-impossible feat for even a brilliant and ambitious young man. So many exciting things were happening, so many splendid and nefarious projects were being undertaken and carried out, that only the most spectacular performances could win much attention. In 1586 came the news of Sidney's heroic death at Zutphen; a year later Mary of Scotland was executed; another year later the Spanish Armada was destroyed. Through all the scenes of public sorrow, terror, and rejoicing of those years, through all the horrors of the great plague of 1592-1594; while Marlowe swept London off its feet with his bombastic tragedies and came to his sordid end, while Kyd and Spenser and Lyly were creating new literary fashions of extraordinary popularity, while Nashe and Greene were exploiting the melodramatic life of the gutters and gangs, Milton remained in obscurity.

Shakespeare, as we know, lost little time in discovering a means of livelihood and a congenial profession. He invaded the theater and, in the face of jealous opposition, swiftly made his way as actor, poet, and playwright, so that within a few years his *Richard III*, *Romeo*, and *Midsummer Night's Dream* had established him in the front rank of writers of histories, tragedies, and comedies. Milton lacked the transcendent energy necessary for any such accomplishment. But one may infer from events

44

subsequent to 1595 that he practiced music and that he maintained contacts with musicians and writers. He could hardly
have failed to associate with George Peele, his colleague of the
days of the Alasco revels, whose *Old Wives' Tale,* a play with
plenty of incidental music, was well received.[1] Since Peele was a
friend of Shakespeare's and is said to have acted with him at the
Blackfriars' Theatre, there is at least a faint chance that Milton
may have met Shakespeare himself as early as this.

But professional opportunities for a young scholar and musician were at this time very scant indeed, since there were no
public concerts and no public support for the art. Unless one
could get a post in a church or in the Royal Chapel or could
manage acceptable overtures to a wealthy patron, one would be
left only to give private instruction at tiny fees or to set an
occasional song for a play or entertainment. Milton may have
survived by turning his hand to such comparatively thankless
jobs.[2]

It is rather likely that he lived as a humble tutor of some sort
and kept up his music in a more or less unprofessional capacity.
He undoubtedly found his way, as a well-mannered and well-
educated youth, into those interesting informal musical soirees
in which so many people were now beginning to find great delight. The most famous of these took place at the home of one
Nicholas Yonge in the parish of St. Michael's in Cornhill.
Yonge, a chorister of St. Paul's Cathedral, was an ardent collector of musical publications. He specialized in the madrigal,
a secular form which was generally of a lighter and more graceful
texture than the familiar *a cappella* motets and anthems, as
befitted its pastoral and amorous words. The Netherlanders and

---

[1] Milton's probable association with Peele was unfortunately terminated by
Peele's death in 1597.

[2] Aubrey (see Milton [3], p. xxii) declared that Milton "got a plentiful estate"
by his music; but it is extremely difficult to see how he could have done so. His
fortune was undoubtedly built up by financial transactions.

Italians had been developing the form for a couple of generations, but it now remained for the English to infuse into it some of their own characteristic elements of boldness and effervescence. Here in Yonge's house, where he lived with his wife Jane and his nine children, musicians of all kinds would meet and talk. Presently they would draw up their chairs to the table; the host would distribute the latest printed part-books, and the company would sing these novel works.

Yonge himself has described these gatherings with engaging simplicity: [3]

Since I first began to keep house in this city, a great number of gentlemen and merchants of good accompt (as well of this realm as of foreign nations) have taken in good part such entertainment of pleasure, as my poor ability was able to afford them, both by the exercise of music daily used in my house, and by furnishing them with books of that kind yearly sent to me out of Italy and other places.

The historical significance of these intimate exercises was indicated in the Armada year of 1588, when Yonge published a large collection of Italian madrigals with English translation, called *Musica transalpina*. It was the first publication of its kind in England. It consisted chiefly of works by the most celebrated foreign masters, including Palestrina, Marenzio, and Orlando di Lasso, but it contained also sixteen examples by the elder Alfonso Ferrabosco, who had settled in England as early as 1562, and two by William Byrd, who must have been a welcome visitor at Yonge's house.

Since the death of Tallis, in 1585, Byrd was, for Englishmen, the acknowledged "Father of Music," and it was he who actually inaugurated the astonishing outburst of Elizabethan madrigals, an outburst upon which still rests England's chief claim to musical equality with Italy and Germany.[4] A few months after

---

[3] In the Dedication to *Musica transalpina*, 1588.

[4] Despite the earnest efforts of both antiquarians and practical musicians, the superlative character of the English madrigalian period of music is still largely

Musica transalpina had appeared, he published his epoch-making set of *Psalmes, Sonets, & Songs of Sadness and Piety,* "made into music of five parts," and in the following year his *Songs of Sundrie Natures* and the first book of his *Sacrae cantiones.* One of his most accomplished pupils, Thomas Morley, of the Royal Chapel, followed him with books of madrigals, canzonets, and ballets, in 1594 and 1595; and John Mundy continued the fashion with a set of songs and psalms.

The great English musical renaissance had now fairly begun. And since Milton was soon to be associated with Morley in a highly important publication, he must have become known at this time to the masters who have just been mentioned. His own modest efforts probably came to the attention of Byrd himself, and at Yonge's home he may have heard Byrd play the newer revolutionary music for the virginals. He listened with delight to the older man's voluntaries, to his naïve imitative "battle music," to his variations on popular songs, to his grave and sprightly dance tunes.[5] There he also may have sung a part in the latest madrigals: Byrd's, Morley's, and perhaps even his own.

But he could scarcely make a living by such pleasant diversions. He cast about for some more substantial, even if less artistic, method of survival, for he may have discovered what it

---

unrecognized. Sometimes even a connoisseur of the arts goes astray in the mere matter of factual information. For instance, Spaeth (p. 2) says, that "the words were of little importance, and frequently consisted of meaningless phrases repeated over and over." To refute this, one needs merely to read through the splendid text of Gibbons's madrigal book (Fellowes [2] pp. 97-100). Spaeth (p. 3) further declares that the Elizabethans emphasized correctness rather than beauty and (p. 7) that "little or no attention was given to the manner of producing or modifying the quality of tone." This is untrue—although it must not be imagined that all performances of this music were necessarily excellent. Shakespeare's Touchstone was driven on occasion to cry, "God mend your voices!" and "An he had been a dog that should have howled thus, they would have hanged him"—bespeaking the prevalence of some critical sensibilities.

[5] Forty-two specimens of Byrd's early virginal music were written down, as early as 1591, in *Lady Nevell's Book.*

was like to go hungry. Fortunately, as it happened, he had formed an intimate friendship with James Colbron, perhaps a younger man than himself. This Colbron had served his apprenticeship as a scrivener and in 1595 was admitted to the Scriveners' Company. Now the scriveners' profession was a comparatively prosaic one, combining the services that are today performed by attorneys' assistants, law stationers, and notaries, services that were especially important in an age when illiteracy was more prevalent among the well-to-do than it is today.

Scriveners drew up and witnessed wills, leases, marriage settlements, and suchlike legal documents, and they often did some money lending and trading in securities on the side. They were organized into a kind of guild or union called the Company, governed by a master, wardens, and other elected officials. Qualified youths were admitted as members after serving apprenticeship for seven years. By their oath of office they swore "upon the Holy Evangelists" to exercise all possible diligence, care, skill, and above all honesty in the practice of their profession; they bound themselves even to read over the documents they produced for their clients, and, whenever possible, to prevent all double dealing and sharp practice.[6]

Colbron and Milton discussed the situation and finally evolved a solution for Milton's predicament. He was now thirty-two years of age and had not yet made anything like a start in life. The two friends agreed that Milton could do worse than be bound over immediately as Colbron's apprentice. Furthermore, in view of his age and his training, they managed to persuade the officers of the Company to accept from him a reduced period of five years as apprentice, with a money payment as partial compensation.

And so we find Milton, from 1595 to 1600, occupying a

[6] Masson (I, 25-29) discusses fully the scrivener's profession and Milton's association with Colbron.

novice's little stool and pew in the office where Colbron, his junior in years, sat at the master's desk—filing away documents in drawers and pigeon holes and attending to the minor requirements of clients. He may, with luck, have been excused from wearing the usual blue livery of the younger and often riotous apprentices.

We may be certain that Milton did not fail to enliven his existence, during these dull and doubtless exasperating years as an underling, by following with avidity the stirring progress of English music. His acquaintance, Morley, who had now received the printing monopoly formerly in the possession of Tallis and Byrd, was writing his most charming and readable treatise, *A Plain and Easy Introduction to Practical Music,* and was producing dozens of madrigals. New talent was appearing on every side: Farnaby, Wilbye, and a mere stripling named Weelkes were acquiring laurels in these unaccompanied vocal pieces that had become the smartest form of after-dinner diversion in the homes of the well-to-do. And to this great madrigalian outburst was now being added the blossoming of a new art, that of the ayre or solo art song, accompanied by the lute. Such men as Dowland, Cavendish, Jones, and Morley himself were producing scores of these compositions.

To Milton's life as an apprentice and amateur in music was now added another and inevitable element, that of romance. There was living in the city at this time a Mistress Ellen Jeffrey, who had come of a substantial Essex family and had married a London merchant tailor, Paul Jeffrey. He had died in 1583, leaving her with two daughters, Sarah, aged ten, and Margaret. The widow was well-to-do. Somehow Milton formed an acquaintance with this respectable family, possibly through his legal work in Colbron's office, and he fell in love with Sarah, now grown up to young womanhood. The romance prospered and waited only for the suitor's establishment in his profession.

Finally the year 1600 arrived, the most eventful single year in Milton's life. On the twenty-seventh of February, according to the books of the Scriveners' Company, "John Milton, son of Richard, of Stanton, Co. Oxon, and late apprentice to James Colbron, Citizen and Writer of the Court Letter of London, was admitted to the freedom of the Company." [7] At last, and in his thirty-seventh year, when his contemporary Shakespeare had already written half his plays, Milton was ready to embark seriously upon the beginnings of his career.

He lost no time in marrying Sarah Jeffrey, she being then twenty-eight, nine years his junior.[8] The Widow Ellen was left with her younger daughter Margaret. Whatever vexation Milton may have felt at his belated fortunes was balanced by his satisfaction in now discovering his wife to be a most kindly and helpful person. Years later their poet-son John was to characterize her[9] as "a most excellent mother, known for her charities throughout the neighborhood." The only deficiency that posterity has been able to discover in her is that she had very weak eyes and was compelled to use spectacles from her thirtieth year onward. But however her appearance might have been damaged thereby, her husband was able to remedy any practical difficulty for her, for we know that he was still reading without spectacles in his eighty-fourth year.

The Miltons quickly found a satisfactory house in which to live and conduct business. It was of the usual timber and plaster construction and was located in an excellent neighborhood, in Bread Street, which, as John Stow the London annalist had described it only two years before, was "now wholly inhabited

---

[7] See Masson, I, 25.

[8] Masson (I, 30-39) presents the complex story of the discovery of the facts about Milton's marriage, giving major credit to Col. J. L. Chester, whom he calls a "Hercules of Genealogy."

[9] In his *Denfensio Secunda*, 1654. Milton (3), p. 1145.

A DOCUMENT WITNESSED AND SIGNED BY MILTON AS SCRIVENER

Beginning and end of a manuscript in the collection of muniments at Dulwich College. Assignment of a lease, January 21, 1606/7, by Richard Scudamore of London to Tho. Calton of Dulwich, for the sum of £40, to be paid "Att the now shop of John Mylton, scrivener, in Breadstreet in London." "Sealed and delivered in the presence of Jo: Milton: Scr."

by rich merchants." [10] Milton must have acquired at least a modest sum, perhaps from Colbron, perhaps from his mother-in-law, in order to make such an enviable beginning.

Bread Street, at a distance of only three houses to the north of the Milton home, opened into Cheapside or West Cheap, one of the great thoroughfares of the metropolis, lined with the shops of poultrymen, mercers, and goldsmiths, crowded during the day with pedlars crying their wares; sprats, haddocks, mutton pies, walnuts, ink, oysters, gooseberries. Here the rat catcher and the chimney sweep and the chiropodist and the maimed beggar carried on their various business, until the watchman made his rounds, chanting, "Twelve o'clock, look well to your fire, your lock, and your light." Here also the elaborate city processions and pageants were held. Not far away from the Miltons' dwelling was the celebrated Mermaid Tavern, where pipes were smoked, and Canary was drunk, and repartee was exchange by Shakespeare, Ben Jonson, Beaumont, Fletcher, and other wits, including possibly Morley and Milton. Two parish churches stood in Bread Street itself, St. Mildred the Virgin, and All-hallows, where Milton was to worship every Sunday and where some of his children's christenings and funerals were to take place.

Milton named his own house the Spread Eagle and hung over his door the usual sign to indicate his place of business, since house numbers were unknown at that time. The name and the device for the sign were obviously suggested to him by the arms of the Scriveners' Corporation, which contained a spread eagle, "holding in his mouth a penner and inkhorn and standing on a book." His son John was later to use a variation of this device on his small silver letter seal, which is still in existence. As his business flourished in the years to come, the elder Milton, like

[10] *The Survey of London,* by John Stow, Citizen of London, 1598. London & Toronto, J. M. Dent & Sons; New York, E. P. Dutton & Co., 1912. p. 309.

Shakespeare, successfully applied for an official grant of arms, which was properly recorded by Sir William Segar, the Garter King-at-Arms after 1603.[11] Thus the Miltons finally broke into the ranks of recognized gentlefolk.

The Spread Eagle itself was destroyed in the great fire of 1666, but there is no difficulty in visualizing its main features. Within the entrance was the business office, with chairs for clients and desks for the master and his assistants. To the rear was a living room, furnished with a dining table, with books and music, and the kitchen; in the upper story, with its gable projecting over the street, were the sleeping apartments. Here Milton was to live for the next thirty-two years.

Domestic misfortunes soon saddened the new household. In 1601 the first child was born, designated in the records as a "crysome" infant—meaning that it died before it could be baptized. In this year also the bereaved parents must have received some word of Richard's stubborn recusancy and his punishment. Probably the door would have been gladly opened to receive him, since he was then approaching his seventieth year, but no word has come to us to indicate that the old yeoman ever unbent or accepted a reconciliation with his son. He remained a bitter adherent to the Popish tenets to the end.

Material prosperity, however, served to counterbalance such sorrows and anxieties to some extent. No one has ever contradicted the junior John Milton's statement [12] that the scrivener was a man of the utmost integrity, and in his case, at least, virtue seems to have been more than its own reward. There are records of business transaction during his early professional years, including documents executed in the Spread Eagle office, which indicate that he employed at least one servant, Peter Jones, and presently an apprentice of his own, William Bolde. Two of these

[11] Masson, I, 5-7. The poet's seal has been reproduced on the cover and the title page of Milton (3).

[12] See note 9.

documents, a copy of a bond and an assignment of a lease, are attested by his own signature—they are the earliest extant specimens of his handwriting.[13] Soon he was the outright owner, not only of the Bread Street house, but also (according to Aubrey) of "another house in that street, called The Rose, and other houses in other places." The considerable fortune that he amassed in time was probably the result of an extended series of wise investments in city real estate.

But, as Phillips has engagingly observed, his business did not compel him "so far to quit his own generous and ingenious inclinations, as to make himself wholly a slave to the world; for he sometimes found vacant hours to the study (which he made his recreation) of the noble science of music. . . . He gained the reputation of a considerable master in this most charming of all the liberal sciences." [14] He installed an organ in his house and played on it frequently, using the voluntaries of Blitheman, Byrd, Bull, and Weelkes. Like other musically inclined gentlemen, he also owned a lute and a pair of virginals and undoubtedly a "chest of viols," consisting of six of these instruments, of various sizes. Among his extant compositions are several fantazias for viols,[15] such compositions as he and his family and visitors to Bread Street must have played often in the back room of the Spread Eagle.

We now turn again to the eventful year of 1600, for it was then that, by an ironical stroke of fortune, Milton's musical talents were strikingly recognized—at almost the very moment when he had irrevocably committed himself to his career as businessman. This recognition came through Thomas Morley, now

[13] Lansdowne MS. 241, f.58; f.363. These are embedded in the diary of John Sanderson, a Turkey merchant, and are dated 1603; the assignment of the lease, dated January 21, 1606-7, is found in the collection of muniments at Dulwich College. See Masson, I, 5n; and a communication from George F. Warner in the *Athenaeum*, March 20, 1880.

[14] Milton (3), p. xxxii. Quoted by Arkwright, Memoir, p. 7.

[15] In the library of Christ Church, Mus. MS. 423-428. See pp. 142-143.

England's foremost madrigalist. One day Morley arrived at Bread Street with important news and a fascinating proposition. Charles Howard, the Earl of Nottingham and Lord High Admiral, had decided that the Queen needed some novel form of entertainment. Elizabeth was now in her sixty-seventh year, beset with troubles and the physical frailties of her age and unable to undertake such strenuous royal progresses as those she had always delighted in. Plays and bearbaiting she still enjoyed, but what would now appeal to her more would be some gentler and more artistic form of amusement. What about a cheerful musical project, in the form of a great tribute from the best composers of the realm? The Earl had conferred with Morley, and together they had developed the scheme for the "Triumphs of Oriana."

The idea was suggested in the first place by a publication which had appeared in Venice eight years before, called *Il trionfo di Dori.* This consisted of twenty-nine madrigals for six voices, by Marenzio, Giovanni Croce, Anerio, Palestrina, and other composers. Each madrigal ended with the refrain, "Viva la bella Dori." The *Trionfo* had become immensely popular and was going through many editions, not only in Italy, but also in the Netherlands and Germany.[16] Croce's contribution had been reprinted, with English words, by Yonge in the second book of *Musica transalpina,* in 1597.[17] A further hint was obtained from a madrigal by Michael Cavendish in his set of 1598, entitled "Come, gentle swains," and ending with the refrain, "Long live fair Oriana." [18]

It is not known whether Cavendish originally intended his "Oriana" to represent Elizabeth, but Morley and Nottingham felt that no name could be more appropriate for their project. It

[16] See Grove, art. *Trionfo di Dori,* by Fuller Maitland.

[17] This madrigal appeared also in the *Triumphs of Oriana* as "Hard by a Crystal Fountain." One of Morley's settings makes use of the same words.

[18] See Fellowes (2) pp. 381, 611.

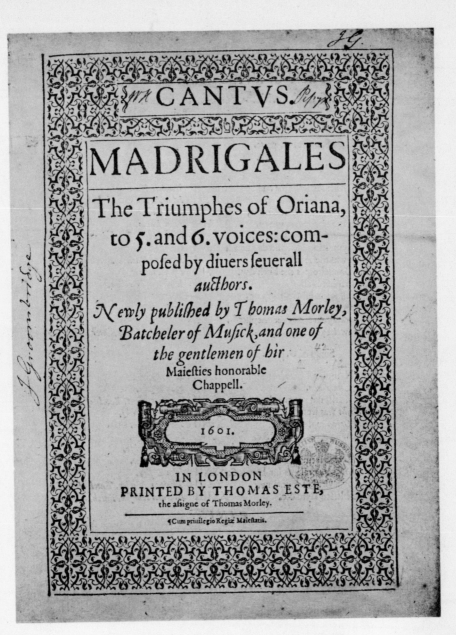

TITLE PAGE FROM THE CANTUS BOOK
"THE TRIUMPHES OF ORIANA"

was the name of the heroine in the Castilian romance of Amadis of Gaul, recently popularized in England by Anthony Munday's translation, and it was sufficiently close to Spenser's own "Gloriana" of the *Faerie Queene*. At any rate, the two schemers decided to invite the leading English musicians to contribute madrigals to a new collection to be called *The Triumphs of Oriana*. Each composition was to end with the refrain, "Then sang the shepherds and nymphs of Diana: 'Long live fair Oriana' "; and the work was to be designed for the Queen's particular honor.

The already completed pieces of Croce and Cavendish were to be rewritten and used, and Morley himself agreed to write two, as well as to superintend the venture. Composers were approached, both in London and elsewhere, and soon there were in hand contributions by a most imposing list of artists, including Wilbye,[19] Weelkes, Thomas Tomkins, Robert Jones, Kirbye, Ellis Gibbons, Farmer, John Mundy, and Bennet. Only two of the most celebrated madrigalists were missing from the complete list. One was Byrd, Morley's master, who was probably harassed by lawsuits at the time, and troubled with prosecutions as a recusant.[20] The other was Giles Farnaby, who is on this account supposed to have died around 1600; but this is unlikely. The absence of lutenists such as John Dowland and of keyboard virtuosi such as John Bull, who had written few if any madrigals, needs no explanation.

That Morley came to Bread Street and invited Milton to join in this important and elaborate undertaking is of considerable importance. Morely could hardly have asked him

[19] Wilbye's contribution became so famous that the whole collection was sometimes ascribed to him rather than to Morley. This would account for Phillips's curious statement that three or four of Milton's "songs" were "still to be seen in the old Wilby's set of Airs." Aubrey mentions "Wilby's Set of Orianas." See Milton (3), p. xxxii; and Selected Essays . . . by John Milton, edited by L. E. Lockwood, Boston, Houghton Mifflin Co., 1911, p. xlii.

[20] See Fellowes (3), pp. 19-30.

unless he had already given unmistakable evidence of talent and skill in the composition of light secular music. No mere novice could have been permitted to approach the Queen herself, in a public tribute, and in such august company. Yet Milton's Oriana piece is the only madrigal of his which has been preserved to us. Nobody knows what became of the manuscripts of the others that he must have composed. Future exploration may yet reveal some of them; they would probably prove very well worth searching for, if we may judge their quality by the single one we have.

The verses Milton used are as follows: [21]

> Fair Orian, in the morn
> Before the day was born,
> With velvet steps on ground,
> Which made nor print nor sound,
> Would see her nymphs abed.
> What lives those ladies led!
> The roses, blushing, said:
> O stay, thou shepherds' maid.
> Then on a sudden all
> They rose and heard her call.
> Then sang those shepherds and nymphs of Diana:
> Long live fair Oriana!

Whether Milton is to be credited with the words as well as the music no one can say, since the authorship of none of the Oriana verses was divulged. But the fact that he used these comparatively light and indeed frivolous lines argues that he was by no means a man of dour "puritanical" leanings, as has sometimes been supposed.

Four voices only are employed for the sprightly opening of the composition, singing with freshness and vigor. At the

---

[21] Fellowes (1), pp. 186, 247-249; Fellowes (2), pp. 149, 269. The most useful and reliable edition of the entire words and music of the *Triumphs* is Vol. xxxii of the English Madrigal School, in which Milton's *Fair Orian* occupies pp. 189-198.

words, "with velvet steps on ground," all six parts are engaged, probably very softly. It is amusing to note what rol-
licking verve is thrown into the music for the naïve exclamation,
"What lives those ladies led!" And the rest of the composition,
with its sudden turn toward wayward romance at the words,
"The roses, blushing, said: O stay, thou shepherds' maid," and
with its exhilarating conclusion, all carried out with great
contrapuntal skill in leading the six voices, is surpassed only
by the contributions of Morley and Wilbye and by Weelkes's
sheer masterpiece, "As Vesta Was from Latmos Hill Descending." [22]

Morley was undoubtedly pleased when Milton showed him
what he had accomplished, and it is possible that "Fair Orian"
was first performed for a select group of friends at the Spread
Eagle. There can be little doubt, too, that there was a Court
performance of the whole series some time before the summer
of 1601. Morley, Milton, and such of the other Oriana composers as were in London were probably presented to Elizabeth by the Lord High Admiral; a company of six good
singers was brought in, and the Queen was cheered by this compliment to her person and this novel expression of the good will
of her subjects. One would like to know whether it served to
bring her some much-needed solace, for she had just experienced
all the ghastliness of the execution, by her own warrant, of
her unfortunate favorite, the Earl of Essex. Concerning the
ambitious scrivener's pleasure in the event there can be no question.

The Oriana collection was made ready for publication, under Morley's editorship, in 1601, together with a fashionably
euphuistic dedication to Nottingham. But although the date
1601 appears on the title pages of all of the six part-books in

[22] Since the score of Milton's composition is available in several modern editions,
it will be unnecessary to present more than one illustration from it. The conclusion
of the madrigal may be consulted on pp. 165-167, Example 1.

which it was printed, it was not actually issued to the public until 1603, according to the Stationers' Register.[23] "Oriana" herself did not live long enough to take joy in the printed edition. There were two editions in the year of her death, and presently a few more detached Oriana pieces were composed, in a somewhat sadder vein. Two appeared in Bateson's madrigals, of 1604, and in one of these the refrain is changed to "In Heaven lives Oriana." The same change is found in one by Pilkington in his 1613 set. Finally Thomas Vautor, one of the last of the madrigalists, included in his *Songs of Divers Airs*,[24] in 1619, a setting using the lines, "For Oriana is not dead, but lives renowned," and "Sing then, ye shepherds and nymphs of Diana: Farewell, fair Oriana."

The *Triumphs*, because of its interesting historical associations, has enjoyed a greater vogue in modern times than any other contemporary collection of English vocal music. Musical historians have given it perhaps more notice than they should, since they have often slighted other works of at least equal merit. To be sure, it shared the obscurity and the contempt that enshrouded all but a pitifully small portion of Tudor and early Jacobean work throughout the eighteenth century. But its various numbers have been kept alive through the performances by British singing societies ever since 1814, when William Hawes brought out the first of a long series of modern reprints. While Milton's other music has lain forgotten in manuscripts at the British Museum and Christ Church, his "Fair Orian" has at least been heard by many hundreds of persons during the last century.

One more speculation of interest remains to be considered before we proceed to chronicle the events following the fortieth

---

[23] See Grove, art. *Triumphs of Oriana*, by Fuller Maitland. According to Davey (p. 197) the Earl of Devonshire bought a copy in December of 1601.

[24] English Madrigal School, Vol. xxxiv, No. 22: "Shepherds and Nymphs."

Ayre *Ori an* in the morne, in the morne, before the day was borne, with

veluet steps on ground, which made nor print   nor sound, which: ij.   nor soud,

Would see hir Nymphs a bed,   what liues those Ladies led, what: ij.

what: ij.   those: ij.   what: ij.   The Roses blushing sayd,

O stay,   O stay thou shepherds mayd, O stay: ij.   And on a sodain all they

rose and heard hir call, they: ij.   they: ij.   Then sang those

shepherds and Nymphs of *Diana,*   and Nymphes: ij.   Long liue faire

O-ri ana, Long: ij.   Long: ij.   Long: ij.   I. L.

TENOR PART OF MILTON'S "FAIR ORIAN"

year of Milton's life and the accession of James I. Masson
has toyed with the tempting notion that Shakespeare, on his
last recorded visit to London, in 1614, walking down Bread
Street after a boisterous session at the Mermaid, may have
paused before the Spread Eagle to gaze wistfully at a fair
child of six—at John, the son of the scrivener.[25] Far more
likely than such a chance encounter is the possibility that the
dramatist had already met the elder Milton as early as 1601
through Thomas Morley.

Thomas Morley is one of the extremely few contemporary
musicians whose compositions are known to have been actually
played and sung at an original performance of a Shakespeare
play. The song, "It was a lover and his lass," used in *As You
Like It*, early in 1600, immediately appeared with its music,
in Morley's *First Booke of Ayres or Little Short Songs, to
Sing and Play to the Lute*, in the same year.[26] Besides this
unique record of collaboration, there is the notation in the
Rolls of Assessments for Subsidies, of Bishopsgate, between
1596 and 1601, that the goods of Morley and Shakespeare
were assessed at the same amount.[27]

There is thus an enticing possibility that the musician and
the playwright were more or less closely associated; and if
it ever became necessary for either or both of them to produce

---

[25] Masson, I, 45-46.

[26] The unique surviving copy of this book was for many years inaccessible to
scholars, having been stored away by Henry C. Folger. Consequently many badly
garbled versions of the music to the Shakespeare song were circulated. After the
establishment of the Folger Shakespeare Library, in Washington, Fellowes pro-
cured a photostatic copy of the whole work and reprinted it as Vol. XVI of the
English Lutenist School (London, Stainer and Bell, 1932).

[27] Bridge, p. 25n, quoting Arkwright. See also Fellowes's *Introduction* to Morley (1), p. vi. The inference that both the poet and the musician "appealed"
against the assessment is not accepted by M. S. Giuseppi (Transactions of the
London and Middlesex Archeological Society, n.s., London, 1929, V, 283-287),
who holds that the notation "affid" before their names indicates simply that the
collectors testified that the sums due in the assessment had not been received.

legal documents, they might very readily have engaged the services of the musical scrivener of Bread Street. Shakespeare's interest in music, attested by his not less than 500 references (some of them highly technical) to the art, adds considerable weight to these suppositions.[28] London, with its population of a mere 200,000, was at this time a small place as modern cities go, and the opportunities for close association between persons interested in similar pursuits were much greater than they are in the Paris, New York, Rome, Vienna, or London of today. One may therefore be forgiven for imagining that England's greatest poet might have spent some few pleasant hours, at one time or another, with the composer of "Fair Orian."

[28] See *Shakespeare, His Music and Song*, by A. H. Moncur-Sime. Third edition, London, Kegan Paul, Trench, Trubner & Co. (n.d.), p. 19. See also Naylor (3).

CHAPTER IV

Lamentations of a Sorrowful Soul

1603-1614

THE AS-YET-CHILDLESS household in Bread Street had welcomed a new member in 1602. In that year Margaret, the younger daughter of the widow Ellen Jeffrey, had married a substantial widower from Essex, William Truelove. The scrivener, acting as the son-in-law of Mistress Ellen, had attested her formal consent to the marriage. This consent may have cost her at least a gentle pang of regret, for the newly married couple were to leave London forthwith. Master Truelove owned various properties, not only in Essex, but also in Hertfordshire and elsewhere. He eventually settled with his bride at Blakenham-upon-the-Hill, in Suffolk.

Since the widow was now left completely alone, she was invited to live with the Miltons at the Spread Eagle. She stayed there for the remainder of her life, apparently on the most amicable terms.[1] Soon she was to share in the rejoicing that doubtless greeted the birth of her grandchild Anne, some time before 1607, and of the handsome infant John, on the ninth day of December, 1608.

Thomas Morley did not long outlive Oriana herself; he died in the autumn of 1603. But the remarkable stream of English musical publications continued to flow with full vigor all through the first decade of King James's reign, while Shakespeare's tragic and poetic powers had reached their full maturity and while Francis Bacon and Ben Johnson did their most

[1] Masson, I, 39, 63.

enduring work. The artistic renaissance had reached its most glorious stage. In no field was this more apparent than in music. Masses and motets, services and anthems, madrigals, canzonets, and ballets, ayres, and lute music, extended works for organ and virginals, fantasias for viols, and miscellaneous pieces for various combinations of voices and instruments, all gushed forth in almost unbelievable profusion.[2] No one has yet attempted to compute the total number of compositions produced by English musicians between 1590 and 1620, but it must lie somewhere in the neighborhood of five thousand. What is still more remarkable is the small number of weak or inept works among all of these that have been recently examined and published.

Every good London household cultivated its domestic music, and Milton, now having been publicly accepted into the company of the professionals, exchanged compositions with them and practiced his art both while dispensing hospitality at the

[2] The principal musical publications of these years may be noted here. The following list is by no means complete, and of course it does not cover the hundreds of pieces that survive in manuscript collections.

1603: Dowland, *Third Books of Ayres.*
1605: Hume, *Musical Humours* (ayres and instrumental pieces); Pilkington, *Ayres*; Dowland, *Lachrimae* (instrumental pieces); Byrd, *Gradualia*, Book I (motets).
1606: Danyel, *Songs* (ayres); Bartlett, *Ayres;* Coperario (Cooper), *Funeral Teares* (ayres and duet).
1607: Ford, *Music of Sundry Kinds* (chiefly ayres); Hume, *Poetical Music* (ayres and instrumental pieces); Jones, *Madrigals;* Byrd, *Gradualia*, Book II (motets).
1608: Jones, *Ultimum Vale* (ayres).
1609: Ferrabosco, *Ayres*; Jones, *Musical Dream* (ayres); Wilbye, *Madrigals*, second set; Ravenscroft, *Pammelia* and *Deuteromelia* (rounds).
1610: Jones, *Muses' Garden for Delights* (ayres).
1611: Byrd, *Psalms, Songs, and Sonnets* (madrigals); Byrd, Bull, and O. Gibbons, *Parthenia* (virginal pieces).
1612: Dowland, *Pilgrim's Solace* (ayres); O. Gibbons, *Madrigals and Motets.*
1613: Campion, *Ayres,* first book.
1614: Leighton, *Teares* (psalms & anthems by various composers).

Spread Eagle and while receiving it in other houses. Nicholas Yonge continued his intimate musicales until his death in 1619. Byrd, now in his sixties, was everywhere greeted with affection and venerated as *homo memorabilis*. Milton probably entertained him, in spite of his Roman Catholicism; and he certainly associated with the other Oriana men, such as John Mundy and Robert Jones. Through Jones he met Philip Rosseter, instructor of the children for the Queen's Revels, and Thomas Campion, the poet-musician and physician.[3] Ellis Gibbons, who had contributed two pieces to the *Triumphs*, introduced him to his younger brother Orlando, the inheritor of the mantle of Byrd and Morley, who was to place his compositions beside Milton's in later collections.

Then there were a few rather odd characters to whom he was drawn through his music: John Bull, his fellow pupil with Blitheman many years before, who was now astonishing the Court with his virtuosity; John Dowland, who lived in Fetter Lane after 1605, famous equally for his personal gaiety and for his doleful music;[4] Nathaniel Giles, master of the Royal Chapel children, who carried on the good old tradition of kidnapping and impressing likely boys; and finally that arch-eccentric, Tobias Hume, soldier of fortune, musical innovator, and madman.[5]

Of greater significance, particularly for the story of his son's future development as a poet, is his association with the Italian colony of musicians in London, which was now begin-

[3] All the known facts about Campion, and his complete literary output, are to be found in Campion's *Works*, edited by Percival Vivian, Oxford, Clarendon Press, 1909. His ayres have been reprinted in *The English School of Lutenist Song Writers* (London, Stainer and Bell) and elsewhere.

[4] Dowland's "Lachrimae," called a "passionate pavan," was one of the most popular compositions of the time. Many arrangements of it survive, for virginals, lutes, and voices; and Shakespeare alludes to it several times.

[5] For a brief sketch of Hume's extraordinary career see Warlock (1), pp. 82-90.

ning to play an important part in English artistic circles.[6] These Italians, through their interest in the newer operatic fashions of their fatherland, were doing a good deal to displace the traditions of polyphonic vocal composition with the ideal of the personal, passionate, and dramatic solo song. Their increasing prominence marks the beginning of the submission of English musicians to foreigners, Italian, French, and German, which was to stifle native talent until the late nineteenth century. That Milton looked with some distrust upon their work may be indicated by the fact that he apparently never composed a note according to the newer fashion; but there is also ample evidence that he gladly cultivated them and listened to their compositions with courtesy and interest, if not with delight.

Their leader was the second Alfonso Ferrabosco, court musician under Elizabeth and music tutor to the children of James. He was to be associated with Milton in a famous collection of pieces in 1614. Meanwhile his influence was becoming particularly marked in the courtly form of quasi-opera or entertainment known as the "masque." Ferrabosco had composed the incidental music for Jonson's comedy of *Volpone;* he followed this with a close collaboration with Jonson and Inigo Jones in the production of the most famous and magnificent masques of the time: *The Masque of Blackness, The Masque of Beauty, The Masque of Queens,* the masque for Lord Haddington's marriage in 1609: *The Hue and Cry after Cupid,* and several others. The intimate friendship that developed between this composer and Jonson was eloquently acknowledged by the dramatist in his "Description" of *The Masque of Hymen*[7] and also in the poem *To My Excellent Friend Al-*

---

[6] A pointed discussion of Milton's relations with Italian musical families is found in Smart, pp. 94–97.

[7] Composed for the marriage of Lord Essex and Lady Frances Howard, in 1607. The passage in question was omitted from the Folio edition of 1616, but is quoted

fonso Ferrabosco, printed in the composer's book of *Ayres* in 1609.[8]

One of the most ardent Italians of the time was Giovanni Coperario, who had been born and baptized in England as plain John Cooper, but had visited Italy in 1600 and had come back thoroughly Latinized. In adopting a foreign name he instituted a droll and abject fashion that has lasted to the present day. Coperario worked with Bull and Giles in preparing the music for the feast of the Merchant Tailors in honor of the King in 1607, and received £12 for his songs. He composed the music for Beaumont's *Masque for the Inner Temple and Gray's Inn,* in 1613, and gave lessons at the Court. He was also the music master of the brothers William and Henry Lawes, who were to become such close friends of the Miltons. Another Italian masquer was Nicholas Lanier, who did not change his name, but who married a lady of the Galliardello family. He collaborated with Campion and Coperario in the masque for the Earl of Somerset in 1614.

Quite genuine Italians were also encountered by Milton in this group. There were three musicians, all named Thomas Lupo (probably a pair of cousins and an uncle), one of whom was associated with Giles and Campion in the masque for the

---

by Warlock (1), p. 92: "And here, that no man's deservings complain of injustice (though I should have done it timelier I acknowledge), I do for honour's sake, and the pledge of our friendship, name Master Alfonso Ferrabosco, a man planted by himself in that divine sphere, and mastering all the spirits of music; to whose judicial care and as absolute performance were committed all those difficulties both of song and otherwise, wherein what his merit made to the soul of our invention would ask to be expressed in tunes no less ravishing than his. Virtuous friend, take well this abrupt testimony, and think whose it is. It cannot be flattery in me who never did it to great ones; and less than love and truth it is not, where it is done out of knowledge."

[8] See *The English School of Lutenist Song Writers,* second series, Vol. XVI; London, Stainer and Bell, 1926. The poem is reprinted also in Warlock (1), p. 93. The similar complimentary sonnet by Jonson, found in Ferrabosco's *Lessons for Viols,* 1609, is reprinted in Warlock (1), p. 94.

marriage of Lord Hayes in 1607;[9] the same, or another, Thomas Lupo contributed to the collections in which Milton appeared in 1614 and 1616. Then there was the numerous Bassano family, whose names are encountered with dizzying frequency in the musical annals of the period: Agostino, John Baptista, Jasper, John, Mark Anthony, Andrea, Edward, and Jerome Bassano.

Finally, two younger associates must be mentioned: William Lawes, pupil of Coperario and gentleman of the Chapel Royal; and Thomas Ravenscroft, trained in St. Paul's choir, who at the age of about seventeen (in 1609) had already published two monumental collections of popular rounds and catches. Later he was to call upon Milton for contributions to his *Whole Book of Psalms.*

With these musicians Milton associated on friendly terms after 1603, in his forties and fifties. He was no longer what could be described as a very young man, but his most significant work was still to be done. It was indeed in his forty-eighth year that he turned out a *jeu d'esprit* by which he showed all the youngsters, at Bread Street and at the Court, that the oldsters could still deliver musical miracles—if we may credit a bit of gossip that comes from Aubrey. "I have been told," wrote this sometimes too credulous biographer, "that the father of John the poet composed a song of four score parts for the Lantgrave of Hesse, for which his Highness sent a medal of gold, or a noble present." [10]

This remark has often been dismissed, by Arkwright and others, on the score of Aubrey's general untrustworthiness, and explained away by the supposition that Aubrey was simply referring in a garbled way to Milton's *In Nomine* for Alasco.

[9] The music for this masque has been edited and published by Arkwright: *Old English Edition,* No. 1; London, Joseph Williams, and Oxford, Parker and Co., 1889.

[10] *Brief Lives,* II, 62, quoted by Arkwright, Memoir, p. 5; Milton (3), p. xxii.

It has also been held unreasonable to suppose that the middle-aged scrivener could see fit to waste his time with such a stupendous academic exercise as a composition in eighty real parts. But there is no real evidence which would contradict the statement, and there is some likelihood that Milton did indulge in just this sort of elaborate caprice. If we tentatively accept the remark at its face value, we may easily reconstruct a set of rather entertaining circumstances.

The event happened in the year 1611, when Prince Otto, son and heir of Landgrave Maurice of Hesse, visited England as a suitor for the hand of Princess Elizabeth, eldest daughter of King James. He arrived on the twenty-third of June, with a retinue of thirty persons, and was escorted by the young Count of Nassau. He was a mere boy of seventeen, but "demeaned himself in all things very princely and bountifully." [11] He was entertained by the King, the Queen, and the Prince of Wales, and he visited both Oxford and Cambridge. He received many rich gifts,[12] and doubtless made adequate and munificent return for them. Nor was appropriate musical diversion lacking, for his father, the Landgrave himself, was known as a composer of motets and other sacred music, and, according to Peacham, "was occasionally his own organist." [13] At a Lord Mayor's feast in young Otto's honor, we are told that "an excellent alto sang to the instruments." Presently the youth departed, laden with presents, but unfortunately without the coveted Elizabeth.

Now it is quite possible that, when the arrival of this noble visitor and the various entertainments were topics of general conversation, Milton was reminded of the forty-part *In Nomine*

[11] Stow, *Annales* of 1631, quoted in the account given of the episode by Rye, pp. 143-145.

[12] The gifts are mentioned by Rommell, *Geschichte von Hessen*, Cassel, 1837, Bd. 6, pp. 327-328; also quoted by Rye.

[13] *Compleat Gentleman*, ed. 1622, p. 99.

he had composed under similar circumstances twenty-eight years before. Some of his younger musical cronies may even have twitted him about it in a mild way, and suggested that the day of such sterile curiosities was now past. What could be more natural than for the amiable scrivener to sit down in a semi-jocular mood and produce a musical enormity, twice as complex as the composition of 1583, and send the prodigious score off to his Highness? An amusing triumph it must have been for him to receive again a medal of gold—or at least a noble present of some sort—which, this time surely, had been honorably paid for.

Such jollification as might have resulted from this and similar diversions soon was dampened, however, by further sorrow in Bread Street. The fourth child of the Miltons was born in 1612; with anxious affection it was baptized Sarah, after its mother; and it was buried in the same year. Nor were the parents much more fortunate with their fifth child, again a girl, who was born on January 30, 1614, and named Tabitha; she lived no longer than two and one-half years. These losses were severe blows to the scrivener, visiting him at a time when he felt that he was getting along in years and at an age when the parental affections are said to be especially powerful. They may account in some measure also for the extraordinary care and indulgence which he lavished on his surviving children and for the remarkable fellowship that he later cultivated with his son the poet.

At this time, too, one may safely surmise, Milton's personality was developing increasingly grave and sober characteristics, and he was taking a more and more profound interest in the sharp religious issues of the period. Ever since the accession of James, high-church principles and practices had been making steady progress in government circles, and serious citizens were becoming alarmed. The minister of Allhallows' parish after 1610 was the Reverend Richard Stocke, a Puritan, zealous and anti-episcopal.[14] His probable influence on Milton is not to be lightly discounted. It may be significant, again, that for some of his musical compositions of this period, Milton used, not the text of the "Bishops" or the Authorized Version of the Bible, but a version that seems closest to the Geneva Bible, which retained immense popularity with the pietists and reformers.

One must be very careful, however, not to conclude from such items that the spirit of Puritanism was in any way sapping the artistic exuberance or the natural and cheerful vigor of the musician. The widespread heresy that the more ardent Puritans and Parliamentarians were inveterate enemies of all the joyful arts, particularly of private music, has fortunately been completely exploded by Percy Scholes.[15] It was only in the official music of the church and cathedral that they worked for reform and severity.

We come now to another musical undertaking in which Milton took a large and important part. Its sponsor was a pedantic but colorful person named William Leighton, who was about Milton's age, or a little older.[16] He had been born in Shropshire, but had made his way at the Royal Court, "bearing an axe," as he described it, "in the fellowship of the Honourable Band of Gentlemen Pensioners in Ordinary under two great Princes," [17] namely, Elizabeth and James. In 1599 he had contributed some prefatory verses to a book of harmonized psalm tunes brought out by Richard Allison, a highly gifted composer. On the accession of James he had

[14] *Masson,* I, 55.

[15] In *The Puritans and Music in England and New England,* London, Oxford University Press, Humphrey Milford, 1934.

[16] For biographical details see Pulver, Grove, and the *Dictionary of National Biography*. Of Leighton's life after the publication of the *Teares* nothing seems to be known.

[17] Leighton, Dedication, p. 1.

produced a poem, *Vertue Triumphant, or a Lively Description of the Foure Vertues Cardinal*,[18] in praise of the new monarch. For this astute tribute he was rewarded with a knighthood. Although in the years to come he was undoubtedly an excessively solemn gentleman, he had had certain moments of whimsicality. On one occasion he wrote a humorous four-part ditty entitled *The Deafe Composer of Tunes*.[19]

The characteristic gloom which is now so definitely associated with Leighton was probably the result of a series of misfortunes which began to harrow him in 1608. In that year he was prosecuted for debt by Sir William Harmon, whom he called one of his "hard-hearted adversaries, to whom I was not indebted at all." The courts sided with Harmon, however; in 1610 Leighton was outlawed and otherwise punished, having, as he put it, "for the later days of my age, undergone many extremities and oppressions, of withholding from me many rights, and injuriously forcing me to prison by wrong doing."

His incarceration brought him into a most salutary and pious frame of mind.

Of patience (as of a gentle Mistress) [he wrote] I have learned much, and have had a perfect survey of my self, and the true experience of those certitudes, that the Court and my former prosperous days could not afford, and to vain youth seemed incredible, where coldness of friends, prevailing malice of enemies, strangeness of acquaintance, the sting of sin, the worm of conscience, for by-past vain spending of time and actions, prospecting to nothing but the horrid gulf of hell and everlasting perdition, were presented unto me, and having no other comfort left to prevent desperation, but a hopeful assurance only in the mercies of a mighty and saving God, and so carried into a sea of that supreme bounty . . .

---

[18] A fanciful and pedantic touch in this publication is a wordless canon printed on the title page. The canon was resolved by E. T. Warren-Horne and set to the words, "Resolutio of the Rota . . ." British Museum, Add. MS. 31418, f.70b.

[19] A fragment of this composition, also called *Surdus Melopaeus*, is in the British Museum, Add. MS. 4388, f.84.

And so forth, weeping in high ecstasy, at great length.[20]

Thus it was that he wrote, while in prison, a series of penitential verses and rhymed paraphrases of the Psalms; and in 1613 these were printed in a duodecimo volume entitled *The Teares, or Lamentacions of a Sorrowfull Soule*. The little book enjoyed an immediate popularity, which it indeed merited, for many of the pieces it contained were executed with greater skill and feeling than were the well-known psalms of Sternhold and Hopkins. The increasingly Puritanical temper of the age, too, worked in favor of this mildly glorified doggerel.

Now Leighton fancied himself as a composer as well as a godly poet, and since the fashion of singing the metrical psalms was still on the increase, he hit upon the notion of providing music for his *Teares* by the same method used by Morley in the Oriana project. Eight of the hymns he set himself, in four parts, together with very curious accompaniments for three plucked instruments of the guitar family: the lute, bandora, and cittern. For the remainder he applied to "famous Artists of that sublime profession, where warbling forth of differences of affections, may seem Apollo's infinite silver tuned strings." His loquacity must have been very persuasive, for no less than nineteen of the very foremost musicians responded with contributions.

Most generous of all were the great Byrd himself and our Milton, who provided four compositions apiece. Ferrabosco, Lupo, Jones, and Martin Peerson each contributed three; two each were done by Bull, Coperario, Dowland, Ford, Orlando Gibbons, Hooper, Johnson, Kindersley, Pilkington, Ward, Weelkes, and Wilbye; Nathaniel Giles did one. The total number was fifty-three.[21] Seventeen were called "consort

---

[20] Leighton, Dedication, p. 2.

[21] Fourteen of these pieces were printed in *Sacred Motets or Anthems for Four and Five Voices*, by William Byrd and his contemporaries, edited by Sir Frederick Bridge; London, Novello (n.d.). This collection includes some of the best specimens

songs," since they required four singers, three of whom had to twang an instrument as well as warble;[22] twelve were laid out for four voices unaccompanied, and twenty-four were for five voices. The last group contained the most valuable music in the collection.

Thus Milton, at the age of fifty-one, found himself again in the most illustrious musical company, when the work was finally printed by William Stansby, in 1614. Stansby had apparently determined to do extraordinary honor to the composers and to produce an outstanding specimen of music printing in its most gorgeous and florid aspects. The music was issued, not in a set of small part-books, one for each performer and containing only his part, as the madrigal and motet collections of the time were printed, but all together in a single large volume, eight inches wide and thirteen inches tall. It probably sold for at least eight shillings, or twice as much as the usual book of ayres for voices and lute.[23] The compositions were not arranged in score; but as the book was spread open, all the singers' parts would be found by themselves, facing in different directions, so that the performers could sit comfortably around a table, each one before his own music.[24]

For the "consort songs," the highest, or cantus, part contained also the lute accompaniment, the altus bore the cittern, and the tenor the bandora. In addition, the cantus and bassus notes

---

in the set, by Gibbons, Bull, Dowland, Wilbye, Coperario, and Ferrabosco, as well as by Byrd. But Bridge omits the parts for lute, bandora, and cittern in the consort songs, changes some of the words, and in his Preface observes, mistakenly, that Byrd contributed five numbers in all. None of Milton's contributions are included in this reprint.

[22] Much curious information on such use of instruments is given in the "Note on the instrumental accompaniment of church music in the sixteenth and early seventeenth centuries," in Arkwright, pp. 13-21. Further details are available in F. T. Arnold's *Art of Accompaniment from a Thoroughbass* . . . Oxford University Press, 1931.

[23] See R. Steele, *The Earliest English Music Printing*, London, 1903, pp. 16-17.

[24] This was the method adopted in printing the lutenists' ayres.

TITLE PAGE OF LEIGHTON'S "TEARES OR LAMENTACIONS"

Reduced in size

were to be read by viol players, if available, and the altus by a flautist. This elaborate layout brings to one's mind a most appealing picture of a miscellaneous company of musicians, gathered together after supper in, say, the living room of the Spread Eagle, with the scrivener acting as host and singing bassus, Dowland or Campion playing the lute, others busy with the words or viols or the flute, while the boy John, now six years old, listens politely with his older sister Anne and awaits permission to join in the cantus part himself.

The nine pages of front matter in the book were undoubtedly Leighton's and Stansby's proudest triumph. The title page displays a circular music staff, surrounded by the names of all the contributors and containing four parts of a wordless composition. The bassus part is printed straight in the center, so that this little work can be sung or played by five musicians sitting around the book—when so performed it does make excellent harmony. Within the circle are the royal arms and the crest of Prince Charles of Wales, also the Tudor rose, and the thistle. This whole device is repeated on the second page, containing poetry "in praise of that noble science of music." [25] There follows the autobiographical dedication "To the High and Mighty Charles, Prince of Great Britain, &c," from which we have quoted some characteristic morsels.

Four full pages are given over to further introductory and complimentary verses, by Leighton himself and by some of his poet friends and relatives. Their names are no longer familiar to the general public: Edward Cooke, Antony Dyet, John

---

[25] A couplet in large type at the bottom of this page reads:

> Let this grave Music give your ears content,
> Sith Music's Art is drawn from this concent.

The technical term "concent," meaning harmony of independent musical parts, was employed by Milton the poet in line 6 of *At a Solemn Musick*, possibly having been suggested by its use in such places as this. The word was not "content," as many editors have read it.

Layefield, John Lepton, Arthur Hopton, Luke Jones, Thomas Burt, John Parry, John Moray, Simon Sturtevant, Charles Best. These worthies strained their ingenuity to the utmost. They follow Sir William in punning most impishly on his name: "*Leighton,* our Author's name, from true light floweth;" "Say *Well-i-am* when griefs *Leight on* my part"; "Was ever *Light-on* table set before." They praise his "wondrous skill," his fame "above our modern Poets' flight"; to them he is a "bird of Paradise," although his verse is "lowly and submissive." Sturtevant gambols with an acrostic on the gamut, called "a dodecaedron of the six musical notes, in imitation of David's metrical psalms."

Chiefly they all hail the work as a divine antidote for the poisonous output of recent poets, for their "lascivious, base, and foul unchristian rhymes," for their "forged tales of love and lust." Here is something "to conquer sin, flesh, world, death, Devil, and hell." The last page in the book provides an appropriately fantastic appendix. It contains the title page device and more verse, headed, "The Author, going further in consideration of the incomprehensible power and glory of God, endeth in amazement." Finally, however, there is a quite practical note, to the effect that only one stanza of each poem is printed with the music; performers are urged to supply the remaining stanzas from Sir William's earlier publication. With a little juggling, he adds, the music can also be adapted to other versified psalms.

In view of such advertisement, it is no cause for astonishment that persons who sought in their music a *laborum dulce lenimen* have tended to fight shy of Leighton's *Teares.* This is unfortunate, since the musical content of the book does not maintain continuously the doleful or fanatic mood which seems to be promised. Much of it is graceful, cheerful, and virile. Dr. Burney, writing late in the eighteenth century, could have examined it only superficially when he remarked, "There was, at this time, a kind of maudlin piety, which had seized Christians of all denominations; among Calvinists it exhaled itself in Psalmody; and in others, not less dolorous, in Lamentations. . . . In these Lamentations, whence I shall give one that was set by Milton's father, the poetry is too mean and gloomy for any readers but modern Methodists." [26]

Burney reprinted Milton's consort song, a setting of the following stanza:

> Thou, God of might, hast chast'ned me,
> And me corrected with thy rod,
> Wounded my soul with misery,
> And humbled me to know my God.

This is certainly the most solemn, and possibly the dullest, of all the extant music of Milton, and it seems especially so when it is heard or read without the bright instrumental parts designed to add color to it.[27] Burney read it so, and yet he was forced to remark, after printing it with other songs in the collection, "The preceding plates exhibit specimens of the composition of Milton, Dowland, and Ferrabosco, of which, notwithstanding the greater celebrity of the two last musicians, Milton's production is the best, not only in point of ingenuity, but correctness." [28]

The piece is mainly in simple harmony, note against note, but the third and fourth lines contain some strangely eloquent syncopations, and the concluding measures, when sung with delicate expression, can be made most moving. Curiously enough, this was apparently the most widely known composition of Milton's for a long time. Manuscript copies of various dates are to be found in the British Museum, in the library

[26] Burney, III, 135.
[27] The instrumental parts are included in the reprint in Arkwright, pp. 1-5.
[28] Burney, III, 143.

of the Royal College of Music,[29] and even in the National Library at Vienna, with the words in German translation as "Du Gott der Macht hast mich gestraft." [30]

The three other Milton contributions to the *Teares*[31] are written for five unaccompanied voices, and these represent him almost at his very best. Especially admirable is his setting of Leighton's paraphrase of a couple of famous verses from the fifty-fifth Psalm:

> O, had I wings like to a dove,
> Then should I from these troubles fly!
> To wilderness I would remove,
> To spend my life, and there to die.[32]

Here, indeed, is found no moaning or lamentation, but rather a blitheness of spirit, a sincere joy in the Christian idea of escape from a sinful and vexatious world. The composer has seized upon the notion of flying as the fundamental tone of the piece, and this notion he communicates with remarkable skill. It must be sung lightly and swiftly by agile voices, in

[29] MS. 1940 (four part books).

[30] Nationalbibliothek, MS, 19287, ch. xix, l.f., together with a three-part composition by Henry Lawes, *Lord, Judge My Cause*. See Dr. Joseph Mantuani, *Tabulae codicum manu scriptorum in bibliotheca palatina vindobonensi asservatorum*, editit Academia Caesarea Vindobonensis. Volumen X (codicum musicorum pars ii), Vindobonae, MDCCCIC.

[31] All three are reprinted in Arkwright. *O Had I Wings* was reprinted by Hawkins, II, 502-504.

[32] These lines of Leighton's may be contrasted with the same passage as versified in the Sternhold-Hopkins psalters (and later set by Milton to the "Norwich Tune" in Ravenscroft's Psalter):

> But I do say who will give me
> the swift and pleasant wings
> Of some fair Dove, that I may fly
> and rest me from these things?
>
> Lo then I would go far away,
> to fly I would not cease:
> And I would hide myself, and stay
> in some great wilderness.

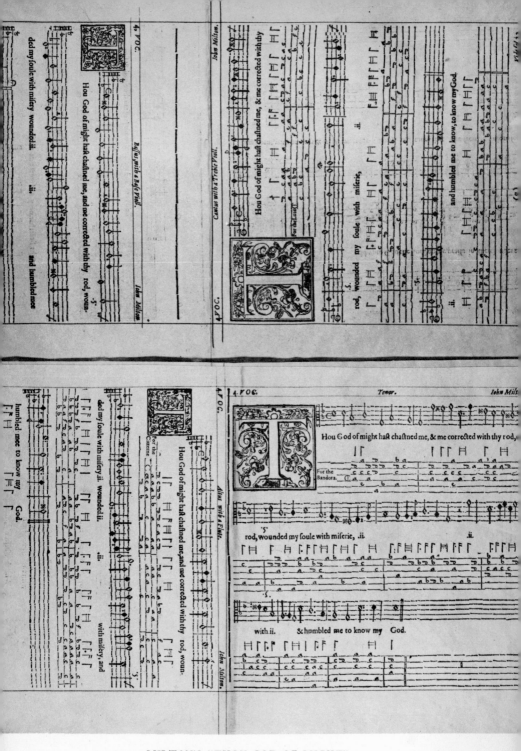

MILTON'S *THOU GOD OF MIGHT*

On two facing pages of Leighton's "Teares," showing the distribution of the parts for the performers seated around a table (reduced to slightly less than half size)

madrigal style; it is really a sacred madrigal rather than an anthem, and it has the typical madrigal structure.

The alto voice leads off with a little skimming phrase, which is taken up by the other parts in succession, chasing one another around in free fugue. Before they have quite finished their flight and pursuit, the soprano sets another figure spinning, to the words of the second line. Thus three subjects are successively dovetailed into one another and whirled about, until the last four words are reached, when there are delicate shifts into more subdued harmonies; and although there is no relaxation in rhythmic pace, the composition ends on a tranquil note. Both Hawkins, who reprinted it in his history,[33] and Arkwright[34] have chosen it as Milton's most admirable essay. He did produce more artful and more inspired works, to be sure, but he never surpassed this one in easy dexterity and purity.

More grave and penitential are his settings[35] of the two following poems:

> O Lord, behold my miseries,
> My pain and deadly grief,
> No help, no hope, but thy mercies
> To yield my soul relief;
> I hate myself and loathe my sin,
> My heart is rent with fear;
> To think what state I have lived in
> My wits with torments tear.
>
> ———
>
> If that a sinner's sighs, sent from a soul
> With grief oppressed, may thee, O Lord,
> To mercy move, and to compassion,
> Then pity me, and ease my misery.[36]

[33] Hawkins, II, 502-504.

[34] Arkwright, Memoir, p. 10; the score is printed on pp. 17-22.

[35] Reprinted in Arkwright, pp. 6-16, 23-30.

[36] It is curious to note that an anonymous poem beginning with the words, "If that a sinner's sighs," but otherwise entirely different from Leighton's, was set by

These compositions are interesting chiefly for their sharp and poignant coloring, deeply expressive of the woeful emotions. The five voices enter successively with each theme as it is introduced and are contrapuntally interwoven, but the most thrilling effects are achieved by means of sudden and surprising harmonic changes and clashes. At the words "No help, no hope," for instance, a major chord is abruptly followed by its minor form, then augmented triads and so-called "false relations," exploiting what is still the most discordant interval known to music. The effect is one of utter despair. Grinding descending imitations among all the voices set off the phrase "with torments tear."

Measures 36-37 of *If That a Sinner's Sighs*, which no editorial revision can smooth out, are (intentionally) harrowing even to the modern ear that can accept Stravinsky or Hindemith,[37] and in measure 59 the three upper voices hold the adjacent notes *C* sharp, D and E in a manner that would seem quite outrageous in its artistic licentiousness, did we not know that composers such as Weelkes and Dowland were also deliberately exploring such adventuresome and forbidding fields.[38] A notably similar effect is used by Weelkes, for instance, in his setting of Psalm 56, at the words, "they keep themselves close."[39] Even Byrd found it necessary to warn the sensitive singers of some of his madrigals to "blame not the printer"

Byrd in his volume of 1588 and also by Dowland in *A Pilgrim's Solace* in 1612. The words are printed in Fellowes (2), p. 46. But Fellowes (2), in his note on p. 255, commits the error of assuming that Milton and Byrd used the same text. Milton even used a *third* poem beginning with the same phrase in his *In Nomine* (see p. 141).

[37] This passage is quoted in Walker, p. 344, as an example of daring, possibly questionable on aesthetic grounds, but typically Elizabethan; see p. 168, Example 2.

[38] Milton's passage containing a "forbidden" simultaneous use of a suspension and its resolution, is presented on p. 168, Example 3.

[39] See Fellowes (1), p. 205.

for passages of this kind, which he intended to sound excruciatingly dissonant."[40]

It is, of course, idle to speculate on the difference it might have made in the course of modern musical history if English composers had continued to develop their art along the lines daringly indicated in such works as these of Milton instead of yielding to the newer homophonic and dramatic styles decreed by continental arbiters of fashion. But the Elizabethan spirit of aesthetic adventure was now entering its decline. It is a matter for irony that Milton, who was doubtless rated as old-fashioned by his younger contemporaries, today sounds surprisingly more "modern" and "radical" than they do. But his contributions to the *Teares*, noteworthy as they were, by no means tell the whole story of his musical accomplishment. Although he was already well over fifty years of age, he was soon to produce even more remarkable works, as we shall shortly see.

[40] *Psalms, Sonnets, and Songs*, 1588, Epistle to the Reader. *English Madrigal School*, XIV, x.

CHAPTER V

The Remedy for Sadness

1615-1618

"*YET ALL THIS WHILE* he managed his grand affair of this world with such prudence and diligence, that by the assistance of divine Providence favoring his honest endeavors, he gained a competent estate, whereby he was enabled to make a handsome provision both for the education and maintenance of his children." So wrote Milton's grandson, Edward Phillips,[1] summarizing with eloquence a great number of important but unexciting events of which there now remain very few records.

We do know, however, that the scrivener had prospered to such an extent, both financially and in the estimation of his business colleagues, that on April 14, 1615, he was elected one of the Assistants of the Company. This election rated him as one of the two dozen leaders in his profession. But he did not serve in his new office for much more than a single year, because of certain political upheavals among the scriveners.

In the latter half of 1616 the Company was required to contribute an assessment which was being levied for the purpose of establishing English colonists in the Irish counties of Coleraine and Londonderry. This project was part of the government's not excessively honorable scheme of forcibly subduing large Catholic districts and supplanting their inhabitants with groups of loyal Protestants. It met with determined opposition on the part of the London scriveners. Some of them, no doubt, felt genuine sympathy for their erring and perse-

---

[1] Quoted Arkwright, Memoir, p. 8; Milton (3), p. xxxii.

cuted Irish brethren. Others may have found it convenient to profess such sympathy, ardent Puritans though they were, since their personal finances were being jeopardized.

Whatever were their motives, the rank and file of the scriveners easily found justification for a flat refusal to pay. They held that the Company could not be legitimately taxed, since it had no official charter of incorporation. The Crown, however, insisted stubbornly on payment and forced the officers, including Milton, to raise the assessment out of their private purses. Smarting under this imposition, and determining to forestall any such further embarrassments, the officers forthwith petitioned the King for a charter under which all members would be equally subject to tribute.

The charter was immediately granted, since the scriveners or "Writers of the Court Letter of the City of London" were held to be "an ancient and honorable society and fraternity, engaged in affairs of great moment and trust." Under this dispensation new officers were elected, including William Dodd as master, Francis Kemp and Robert Griffiths as wardens, and twenty-four liverymen. Milton was not one of these, possibly refusing to serve because of a natural disgust with the hypocrisy and greed that had apparently been exhibited in the dispute.[2]

Meanwhile, on December 3, 1616, on which day he was in the midst of legal transactions, his sixth and last child was born, the third to survive infancy. It was a son, and was baptized Christopher at Allhallows. A bond, drawn up by Milton and witnessed by his apprentice, William Bolde on the day before Christopher's baptism, is preserved in the British Museum.[3] The scrivener was now fifty-two years old; the boy John was seven; the daughter Anne was eight or older.

[2] Masson, I, 61-62. In carrying out the powers granted by their charter, the scriveners presently drew up a revised set of regulations. In January, 1618/9, these regulations received the sanction of Lord Chancellor Bacon and the chief justices.

[3] Harl. MS. Ch. 112, D.19. See the note by George F. Warner in the *Athenaeum*, March 20, 1880.

To the following year belongs the third great collection of music in which Milton appears as a composer, and here his contributions may be justly regarded as his most mature and powerful works. The collection was made by one Thomas Myriell, possibly a clergyman of that name who had come to London from Barnet, ten miles to the north, and had become vicar of St. Stephen's in Walbrook, where John Dunstable, the outstanding musical genius of the early fifteenth century, was entombed. Some of his sermons were published; and in 1622 the musician Thomas Tomkins, one of the Oriana composers, dedicated a sacred madrigal to him.[4] Aside from these meager facts, little is known of his history. Yet this shadowy figure is responsible for one of the most important musical compilations of the whole Jacobean period.

Myriell's work was never published. Its only known copy resides among the musical manuscripts in the British Museum, in the form of six stout part books, of small octavo size.[5] Into these books, designed for the usual singing parts (cantus, altus, tenor, bassus, with the addition of quintus and sextus for five- and six-part compositions), Myriell apparently attempted to write out in his beautifully clear hand the bulk of the significant vocal music of his age, both sacred and secular.[6] Some of it he copied from printed collections, but a great deal he must have obtained by personal application to famous musicians, for many of the compositions in it can be found nowhere else. A few anonymous pieces may be his own productions.

[4] Bridge (p. 38) identifies the clergyman with the compiler of *Tristitiae remedium*. Davey (p. 164) doubts the identification. There is no positive evidence by which either view can be attacked or supported.

[5] Add. MSS. 29372-29377. For description and complete list of contents see the *Catalogue of Manuscript Music in the British Museum*, I, 10-13 (anthems); 281 (motets); II, 150-153 (madrigals); III, 364 (illustration), 390 (carol).

[6] Myriell also owned the manuscript now numbered 3095 in the Fétis Library, at Brussels, which consists entirely of copies of published music. This collection contains his autograph signature, according to Grove.

TITLE PAGE OF MYRIELL'S "TRISTITIAE REMEDIUM"

That he intended the work for publication is apparent from the fact that each part book has an engraved title page, reading *Tristitiae remedium, cantiones selectissimae diuersorum tum authorum tum argumentorum labore et manu exaratae Thomae Myriell, A. D. 1616*. This title is enclosed within a classical design; surmounting it are two seated cherubs, one playing a lute and the other a viol. Between them is a lute with broken strings and the motto, *Peritus non ignorat ordines*. The vast bulk of the compilation bears more eloquent testimony to Myriell's enthusiasm and industry than to his practical sense, for the expense of its proposed publication was undoubtedly prohibitive. Even a wealthy patron would have hesitated to subsidize such a gigantic undertaking.

The compositions included reach the astonishing total of 192—ninety anthems, eighty-one madrigals, twenty motets, and a carol. Some Italian composers are represented, such as Croce, Marenzio, and Palestrina, but the majority are Englishmen, thirty-six in all, including Tye, Tallis, Byrd, Bull, Morley, Orlando Gibbons, Wilbye, Weelkes, Ferrabosco, Lupo, Coperario, Giles, and Ravenscroft. Ten specimens of Milton's work are included: one madrigal, one Latin motet, and eight anthems. These, according to at least one historian,[7] are among the most interesting numbers in the collection.

The madrigal turns out to be the familiar "Fair Orian." Three of the anthems were simply lifted by Myriell from Leighton's *Teares*.[8] There remain, then, six compositions not found elsewhere; the motet and five anthems. Two of these were published by Arkwright, in 1900; the other four have now been scored and heard by the present writer, probably for the first time in three centuries.

[7] Davey, p. 164.
[8] These are "Thou, God of Might," "O Lord, Behold," and "If that a Sinner's Sighs." "O Had I Wings" is not found in the manuscript.

For the motet Milton used the words with which he had doubtless been familiar since his childhood at Christ Church:[9]

Precamur, sancte Domine,
Defende nos in hac nocte,
Sit nobis in te requies,
Quietam noctem tribue.

Deo patri sit gloria,
Eiusque soli filio,
Cum spiritu paracleto,
Et nunc et in perpetuum.

The first quatrain was taken from an old evening hymn, part of which had been used by Robert Whyte in his "Christe qui lux est et dies." [10] The entire hymn, consisting of five stanzas, had been set also by Byrd for five voices singing in the plainest note-against-note style.[11]

Milton's setting[12] is for six voices, in his favorite mode, the Aeolian,[13] which is distinguished by a very flexible system of harmonies and cadences, strange at first to ears accustomed to the "classical" progressions of the eighteenth and nineteenth centuries. It opens with great austerity, the middle voices leading and the outer ones entering with imitations so as to build up an effect of restrained sonority. With the third line of the text a more fluid figure is introduced, and the fourth line closes on a calm and resolute cadence. The unrhymed paraphrase of the Gloria Patri, which was not used by Whyte or Byrd, is distinguished in Milton's setting by considerable energy, the voices following closely on one another's heels and gaining power to the end.

[9] See p. 24.   [10] See p. 18.

[11] *Tudor Church Music*, IX, xxi (text), 279 (score). Pages 306-307 and 308 contain two other four-part compositions by Byrd, entitled "Precamur," but without words.

[12] In Myriell's manuscript it is found in the following folios: i-iv, f.135b; v, f.122b; vi, f.17b.

[13] The final bass note is D, and there is one flat in the signature to indicate that the composition has been transposed up a fourth.

Here Milton's harmony is of the purest mid-sixteenth-century type; it exploits no emotional clashes and could readily pass as the work of Tallis or even of Palestrina. In its rhythmical complication, on the other hand, the piece stands as one of the most illuminating specimens of the advanced methods of the polyphonic period. The composition as a whole is perfectly regular in time, and its time divisions are marked by changes in harmony. But these time divisions, which are indicated by bar lines in modern scores,[14] do not coincide with the rhythmic beats, as they do in the music of succeeding ages. Indeed the most thrilling effects are created by a deliberate system of contrast and clash between the harmonic and time framework and the accents in the individual parts. These parts are again syncopated one against the other, each one following the normal expression of its own words. The proper singing of such music is closely analogous to the proper reading of classical poetry or of Elizabethan blank verse, following the dictates of an underlying regular quantity upon which is erected an endless variety of accentual stresses.[15] This explains why one can never get the true effect of the older vocal music by playing the score on a piano, which reveals only the dull background and gives no idea whatever of the excitement aroused by the subtle and dramatic interweaving of the voices.[16]

Another piece of solid work is Milton's setting of the inspired opening sentence of the Burial Service:[17]

I am the Resurrection and the Life, saith the Lord; he that believeth

---

[14] No bar lines were used in the part books of Renaissance vocal music. The singers were expected to keep together by following the rules of mensural notation, a notation which did not know group-rhythm (indicated by regularly recurring bar lines) as introduced by instrumental music toward the turn of the sixteenth century.

[15] See Warlock (1), pp. 131-132, for a lucid discussion of this point.

[16] For a typical illustrative passage from Milton's "Precamur," see pp. 169-170, Example 4.

[17] The score is printed in Arkwright, pp. 39-48.

in Me, though he were dead, yet shall he live; and whosoever liveth and believeth in Me shall not die for ever.[18]

It begins in the proper funereal manner, its five voices achieving solemnity largely through the use of empty fifths. This mood of dignified desolation presently gives way to one of greater expansiveness and strength. A firm rhythm, felt by all the voices simultaneously, develops almost into a grave dance with the words, "and whosoever liveth and believeth in Me," and the end is magnificently sonorous, calling for the greatest volume of tone of which the choir is capable. In its own way this composition is as impressive as the beginning of Morley's Burial Service,[19] which had commanded the admiration even of Dr. Burney.[20]

One Biblical text that seems to have had a quite extraordinary fascination for Elizabethan composers is that of the lamentation of King David on hearing of the death of Absalom.[21] This intensely pathetic cry was set for voices by no less than seven contemporary musicians besides Milton. In addition, it was set in an abbreviated version as a round for three voices by Henry Lawes, possibly as a result of this younger man's later intimacy with the Milton family. Weelkes's beautiful treatment of it is found in Myriell's collection and in several other manuscripts;[22] Thomas Tomkins's, also in the *Tristitiae remedium*, was published in his *Songs* of 1622, with its dedication "to Mr. Thomas Myriell."[23] In Myriell and in other

[18] Milton took the words from the older Prayer Book, based on the "Great" Bible of 1539. Later versions of the sentence end with the words, "shall never die" (John xi, 25-26).

[19] Printed in Boyce, I, 44-53. [20] Burney, III, 105.

[21] 2 *Samuel*, xviii. 33.

[22] Printed in *A Collection of Anthems by Composers of the Madrigalian Era*, edited by Edward F. Rimbault, London, Musical Antiquarian Society (1846), pp. 135-141. Henry Lawes's round has been printed as No. 38 in the *Euterpe Round Book* (Oxford University Press), p. 17.

[23] *English Madrigal School*, XVIII, 112-123.

SEXTUS PART OF MILTON'S "PRECAMUR"

contemporary manuscripts we find the settings by Farnaby, Bearsley, Ramsey, Michael East, and Richard Deering. In most of these the original scriptural words are slightly altered, so as to read:

When David heard that Absalom was slain, he went up to his chamber over the gate, and wept. And as he went, thus he said: O my son Absalom, would God I had died for thee, O my son Absalom, my son, my son!

Milton's composition[24] is laid out for five voices and is in the Dorian mode. The three middle voices begin the narrative quite unpretentiously—almost casually—but shortly after the treble and bass parts have entered comes a bit of naïve realism: with the words, "he went up to his chamber," a rising scale is introduced in the low registers, working up to the limits of the vocal range. There is a moment of complete and breathless silence after the words, "and wept"; and with the anguished cries of the king the music develops more and more intense feeling, the high notes of the bass portraying the very extremity of despair. Near the conclusion the tenor's lowest register is masterfully used to indicate a complete and subdued abandonment to woe. Nothing less mawkish than this and few things more sincerely eloquent have been produced by any musicians who have sought expression for the darker emotions. Here the true ring of authenticity may well be explained by Milton's own fondness for his children.

More romantic and colorful, if somewhat less deeply felt, is Milton's treatment of David's lament for Jonathan:[25]

O woe is me for thee, my brother Jonathan. Thy love to me was wonderful, passing the love of women, and very kind hast thou been to me, my brother Jonathan.[26]

---

[24] Printed in Arkwright, pp. 31-38.
[25] Myriell, i-iv, f.19b; v, f.7b. Weelkes's setting of the same words (a rearrangement of the text in the Geneva Bible) is also in Myriell.
[26] 2 *Samuel*, i. 26.

At the start there is just the faintest foreshadowing of Wagner's *Tristan* prelude, and quite strangely feminine and Tristan-esque are many of the harmonic combinations that follow. The piece is full of vivid, unexpected progressions, and it uses "false relations" again and again with telling effect. The sentence, "Thy love to me was wonderful," is developed in a lengthy free fugue for the four upper voices, the deep bass being held in reserve so as to dominate all the more imperially the concluding section. The final exclamation is handled with surprising ingenuity, and the whole composition leaves the sympathetic listener thoroughly charmed.[27]

But the artistry of the musical scrivener is revealed in its very fulness in the pair of anthems which use the words of the first two verses of the Lamentations of Jeremiah.[28] They were obviously designed to be sung one after the other without pause, and together they form one gigantic composition—for six voices and in the Aeolian mode. The text that Milton used seems to indicate that he was most familiar with the Geneva Bible, the version most popular for private devotion among the Puritans after its publication in 1560, even though the churches were required to use, first the "Bishops'" Bible, of 1568, and, later, the Authorized Version, of 1611. The words found in the Myriell manuscript are identical with those of the Geneva version, with the single exception of "Lady," which had last appeared in the "Great" Bible, of 1539. They are essentially different from any of the other versions current at the time:

---

[27] Since this composition represents Milton's most mature style, and since none of it has hitherto been scored or published, it is now presented in its entirety, on pp. 171-189, as Example 5. Passages especially noteworthy for their harmonic daring, and not to be regarded as amateurish clumsiness or as misprints, may be heard in measures 5, 11, 18, 27, and 48-51.

[28] Myriell, i-iv, f.138b; v, f.125b; vi, f.20b. William Lawes later produced a setting of "She Weepeth Sore in the Night" as a round for four voices. See the *Euterpe Round Book*, No. 32, p. 15.

How doth the holy city remain solitary (alas), that was full of people. She is as a widow, that was great among the nations and Lady among the provinces.

She weepeth continually in the night, and her tears run down her cheeks. Among her lovers she hath none to comfort her; all her friends have dealt unfaithfully with her, and are her enemies.

The custom of singing the Lamentations on the last three days of Holy Week was a very old one in the Roman Church. The wonderful Latin polyphonic settings by Palestrina were adopted in the Pontifical Chapel in the sixteenth century and have been heard there, with certain others, ever since. In England, the early Elizabethan composers produced several remarkable sets of Latin Lamentations, the most noteworthy being those by Whyte, Tallis, and Byrd. A somewhat more elaborate text was used in these Latin compositions, even the title and verse numbers being set to music.

In Milton's determination to produce a vernacular version, for which there was, of course, no place in the official English reformed rite, we have another illustration of his curiously divided enthusiasms. Artistically, he may be described as almost a reactionary, his sympathies again and again being aroused by the grand and complex traditions of the medieval Church and its music. Politically and ecclesiastically his leanings were unmistakably in the direction of revolutionary Puritanism. Both of these tendencies were fused in his polyphonic treatment of the Geneva text, and such a fusion of the man's deepest interests may well account for his extraordinary success with this composition.

The detailed analysis which the music demands cannot be presented here, since it would be almost meaningless without continual reference to the as yet unpublished score. But a few high lights may be roughly touched upon. Three voices, the cantus, altus, and tenor, entering in succession, manage the opening in beautifully sinuous counterpoint. Then all six repeat the first clause in melodies of immense breadth, combined into harmonies of considerable boldness.[29] The words, "She is as a widow," are introduced by two high voices singing a touchingly plaintive phrase, instantly creating a mood of barren loneliness.[30] The music swells out brilliantly as the full choir reaches the words, "great among the nations," and the first section ends in a stormy outburst of sound. Similar effects and even heightened moments of dramatic tension characterize the second section. A telling little descending figure is used to depict the Lady's tears, and an insistent pounding rhythm develops the words, "all her friends have dealt unfaithfully with her," into a colossal climax.[31] The whole work dies away at the last in touching and subdued harmonies.

All these compositions, completed by the year 1616, show that Milton, although the beginning of his career had been grievously belated, had arrived at an enviable position when Shakespeare died. He had prospered financially, he was bringing up a highly precocious son, he was surrounded by accomplished friends, and he had produced the best of his surviving music. But his career was yet by no means complete. He was to compose some highly interesting work during the next few years, not only in music, but also, strangely enough, in poetry.

He had formed an intimate acquaintance with a man whom Phillips has described as "a fine old Queen Elizabeth gentleman"[32] named John Lane. This Lane was an ambitious poet, but more remarkable for industry than for talent. He pro-

[29] A brief illustration is given on pp. 190-191, Example 6.

[30] The phrase deserves quotation (see p. 192, Example 7).

[31] The powerful entrance of the bass in the following passage marks the emotional and technical culmination of the movement, into which is dovetailed the soft development of the final clause (see pp. 193-195, Example 8).

[32] Phillips, *Theatrum poetarum*, 1675, pp. 111-112; quoted by Masson, I, 56-58. Masson here gives a full account of the association of Milton and Lane.

duced enormously long poems, none of which ever deserved or received printing, although Phillips loyally writes of them in the following worshipful terms: "Had they not had the ill fate to remain unpublished, when much better meriting than many that are in print, they might possibly have gained him a name not much inferior, if not equal, to Drayton and others of the next rank to Spenser." Lane seems to have taken a queer delight in writing continuations of medieval romances, some of which were already interminable. His most readable production was probably his addition to Chaucer's *Squire's Tale*.

In 1617 Lane had completed the bulky manuscript of his appendix, in twenty-six cantos, to Lydgate's *Guy, Earl of Warwick*.[33] This opus he showed or read to Milton, who was so enchanted with it that he was inspired to compose a commendatory sonnet, his only known poetic effort. It is found on the verso of the title page of Lane's manuscript, signed "J. M." and headed *Johannes Melton, Londinesis civis, amico suo viatico in poesis laudem*. As the only surviving verse by the father of the author of *Paridise Lost*, it automatically merits more attention than it could deserve on merely aesthetic grounds. Again, its strangely forced involutions of structure and sound, typical of some of the prose of the time, add to it an interest that its apparent crudity could not command. Its quality has even reminded some readers remotely of Donne.

> If virtue this be not, what is? Tell quick!
> For childhood, manhood, old age, thou dost write,
> Love, war, and lusts quelled by arm heroic,
> Instanced in Guy of Warwick, knighthood's light:
> Heralds' records and each sound antiquary
> For Guy's true being, life, death, eke hast sought,
> To satisfy those which *praevicari;*
> Manuscript, chronicle, if might be bought;

[33] British Museum, Harl. MS. 5243.

Coventry's, Winton's, Warwick's monuments,
Trophies, traditions delivered of Guy,
With care, cost, pain, as sweetly thou presents,
To exemplify the power of chivalry:
From cradle to the saddle to the bier,
For Christian imitation, all are here.

To this friendly tribute Lane responded handsomely when
he wrote a poem entitled *Triton's Trumpet to the Twelve
Months, Husbanded and Moralized*. Its manuscript, completed
by 1621, contains an apostrophe to Milton as a musician, from
which it appears that the scrivener had won some reputation
through instrumental composition. This is a point of considerable
importance, since, with the exception of a few fantasias for viols,
his known musical output consists entirely of vocal works. If
Lane was not merely indulging in exuberant invention (as is
quite possible), we should be very grateful to discover Milton's
pieces for such remarkable orchestral consorts as are described
in the following passage:[34]

At this fullpoint, the Ladie MUSICKES hand,
opened the casements wheare her pupills stand,
to whome liftinge that signe, which kept the time,
lowd organs, cornets, shaggbutts, viols chime,
lutes, cithernes, virginals, and harpsicords,
flutes, violins, and softlie touchd recordes,
bandoraes, orpharions, statlie grave,
otherboes, classhers, sweetest of the thrave,
and everie instrument of melodie,
which mote or ought exhibite harmonie,
did fore the muses all theire coninges spend,
so excellent! as note by ynck bee pennd:
for whie! before the close concludes theire noyses,
in str[i?]ke to all these sweetes, a chirme of voices,
warblinge, dicidinge, tewninge, relishinge,

[34] British Museum, Royal MS. 17, B.xv, f.179b. Reprinted in *Six Lectures on the Recorder*, by Christopher Welch, Oxford University Press, 1911, p. 254n.

THE ELDER MILTON'S SONNET TO JOHN LANE

From Harl MS 5243, British Museum

accentinge, airinge, curbinge, orderinge,
those sweete-sweete partes MELTONUS did compose,
as wonder's selfe amazd was at the lose [close?],
which in a counterpoint mayntaininge hielo,
gann all sum up thus ALLELUIA DEO.

By the time this was written, Milton was fifty-eight years of age, and his son John was thirteen. We shall therefore have to go back a few years and give attention to certain happenings in the Spread Eagle household.

CHAPTER VI

The Whole Book of Psalms

1618-1624

MASSON has drawn a rather touching picture of the Milton household at the time when the poet was a growing boy. He describes the warm and happy home, with peace, comfort, and industry reigning within it. "During the day the scrivener is busy with his clients; but in the evening the family are gathered together, the father on one side, the mother on the other, the eldest girl Anne and her brother John seated near, and little Kit lying on the hearth. Possibly one or two of the scrivener's apprentices lived in the house with him, such an arrangement being then common."

The biographer proceeds to discuss the grave Puritanic piety which was then prevalent among the respectable citizenry of London; and he remarks that in Milton's house there seems to have been "a more than usual affection for Puritanic habits and modes of thought. Religious reading and devout exercises would be part of the regular life of the family. Thus a disposition to the serious, a regard for religion as the chief concern in life, and a dutiful love of the parents who so taught him, would be cultivated in Milton [the poet] from his earliest years."[1]

To complete this picture one must in all justice add that a frank enjoyment of the good things in this life was found completely compatible with the scrivener's recognition of its essential and ultimate subordination to its sequel in heaven. The Puritans have suffered so long under the mistaken popular notion that they despised the refined secular pleasures that it

[1] Masson, I, 50.

becomes imperative to remember that not all their moments were given over to devotional exercises and solemn meditations.[2] And there is ample evidence that the Miltons eagerly embraced rather varied opportunities to cultivate the enjoyment of the worldly arts—painting, for instance, as well as poetry and music.

A young Dutch artist, one Cornelius Jansen, was at this time living in Blackfriars. He had come over from Amsterdam and was attempting to make a livelihood by painting portraits at "five broad pieces a head." Eventually he succeeded in doing several portraits of King James and his children. But one of his first commissions was given him by the scrivener Milton, who was so interested in his work that he ordered a portrait of his son John—an indication of parental affection and personal modesty, as well as of financial prosperity. The painting is still in existence,[3] a clear-cut and sympathetic half-length study of the youthful subject, measuring twenty by twenty-seven inches in its frame. It is entitled "John Milton, aetatis suae 10, Anno 1618," and brings before us the slightly plump physique and features of an amiable and self-possessed boy, with hair cropped rather closely and decked out in a black braided dress with lace frill.

It is well known that even at this early age the younger John Milton was intended by his father eventually to embrace a career in the Church. For this we have the poet's own statement. But the scrivener's mind was not unalterably set on the project, as later events proved. He was fundamentally interested in giving the boy a deep and elegant cultural education, as a linguist, philosopher, and poet. If this ambition was to lead

---

[2] See p. 69.

[3] The portrait is now in the possession of Mr. J. Pierpont Morgan. A reproduction in color appears as frontispiece to I, Pt. 1 of *Milton* (1). Other reproductions can be seen in *The Portraits, Prints, and Writings of John Milton.* by Dr. G. C. Williamson, exhibited at Christ's College, Cambridge, 1908, p. 3; and in Masson, Vol. I (frontispiece).

the youth finally into ecclesiastical channels, as it might have done then with far greater likelihood than at later times, well and good; but humane learning and artistic skill, one may assume, were to be the immediate objectives. When the Jansen portrait was painted, young John had already displayed precocity as a versifier. Many years later, in the *Defensio Secunda*, he wrote, "My father destined me, while yet a little child, for the study of humane letters. . . . Both at the grammar school and also under other masters at home he caused me to be instructed daily." In 1641, while the scrivener was still alive, he declared, "I had, from my first years, by the ceaseless diligence and care of my father (whom God recompense!), been exercised to the tongues and some sciences, as my age would suffer, by sundry masters and teachers, both at home and at the schools." [4] And in the poem *Ad Patrem* he testified that it was at the incitement of his father that he first learned French, Italian, and Hebrew.

Of the boy's tutors one was, according to Aubrey, an Essex Puritan, "who cut his hair short"—whether it was the master's or the pupil's hair which was thus trimmed cannot ever be revealed by the biographer's cryptic sentence. Of another, a Scotsman named Thomas Young, we know considerably more. A Master of Arts of the University of Edinburgh, a zealous Presbyterian and anti-Episcopal, he had settled in or near London around 1612, making his living by assisting Puritan ministers and practicing pedagogy. He may have begun to visit the Milton home in his professional role about the year 1618, being then some thirty years old and married. In 1662 he left England to become the pastor of the congregation of English merchants at Hamburg. By that time the scrivener had already seen his son halfway through St. Paul's school.

[4] From *The Reason of Church Government*, quoted by Masson, I, 67. Milton (3), p. 524.

The poet's biographers have treated his schooling so thoroughly[5] that only its main features need to be mentioned here, and very briefly. The school itself was the successor to the old Cathedral School of St. Paul's and was located in the Churchyard. Its first headmaster had been William Lily, famous for his Latin Grammar. Mulcaster the humanist, who ruled over the institution at the turn of the century, had been succeeded, in 1608, by Alexander Gill, a redoubtable theologian and philologer. Associated with him as submaster, or usher, was his son, Alexander Gill, Junior, reputed to be a rather blustering and reckless fellow. "He had his moods and humours," said Aubrey,[6] "as particularly his whipping fits. Often Dr. Gill whipped Duncombe, who was afterwards a colonel of dragoons at Edgehill fight." The elder and the younger Gill had under their care 153 students, that number having been fixed at the foundation of the school as the number of fishes in the Miraculous Draught. These pupils, all chidren of well-to-do citizens, were elected by the Company of Mercers. Their curriculum extended over a period of from four to six years and consisted of Latin, Greek, Hebrew, grammar, poetry, oratory, and philosophy.

The boy Milton remained at St. Paul's from his twelfth to his sixteenth year and appears to have been an exceptionally industrious youth. He seldom left his lessons to go to bed before midnight, and his father ordered the maidservant to sit up for him.[7] It has been asserted that this close application to his books was the first cause of the damage that eventually robbed him of his eyesight. At the same time, it was at St. Paul's that he formed what was possibly the deepest friendship of his life, with the young Charles Diodati, whose death he was to lament in the most poignant of his elegies, the *Epitaphium Damonis*.

[5] See Masson, I, 73 ff.   [6] Quoted in Masson, I, 82.
[7] Milton (3), p. xxiii.

Charles was the son of Theodore Diodati,[8] a physician who had come to London from Geneva, had married on Englishwoman, had settled and practiced his profession successfully in the parish of Little St. Bartholomew. He had three children in all: one daughter, Philadelphia, and the boys John and Charles. Charles entered St. Paul's in 1614 and remained until 1623, when he proceeded to Trinity College, Oxford. The intense friendship which sprang up between him and the younger John Milton may have served to bring the Milton family into a significant association with other naturalized foreigners in London, among whose numbers there were many professional musicians.

It was during the poet's first year at St. Paul's that his father contributed for the last time to a famous compilation of music: this was Ravenscroft's *Whole Book of Psalms,* published in 1621. It has already been noted that, ever since the middle of the sixteenth century, large portions of the British population had delighted to sing, chiefly in private gatherings, a doggerel rhymed version of the Psalter to simple hymn tunes. The custom originated among the earliest Protestant sects, including the followers of Wycliffe and Walter Lollard; it flourished especially in Geneva[9] and spread rapidly wherever the Roman and established churches did not use their teeth too sharply in suppressing it, as we have seen.[10] Official opposition indeed enhanced the popularity of psalm singing, as an act of defiant or semi-defiant piety as well as an exhilarating recreation. It was, moreover, an exercise that appealed to the musically untaught, when the tunes were sung in unison, without harmony; to the moderately skilled when harmonized simply in four parts; and to those with polyphonic prowess when developed contrapuntally "in reports," as the curious term expressed it.[11]

---

[8] Theodore Diodati was the brother of Jean Diodati, the famous Genevan Protestant divine.

[9] See Terry (2), pp. i-xii.   [10] See pp. 30-31; also Procter, p. 83.

[11] Terry (1), pp. 9-12, 23-25; Terry (3), pp. 7-24.

Various immigrant groups gave new impetus to the custom in England; the woolen manufacturers, for instance, who were mostly Flemish refugee Protestants.[12]

The practice was by no means limited to the more radical Protestants, that is to say, the Puritans in England, although they were naturally its most enthusiastic devotees. Queen Elizabeth had permitted the singing of psalms in parish church services under certain circumstances, as an addition to the prescribed ritual, though not as a substitute for any portion of it. Nor was it, as so often supposed, invariably a doleful, droning, and esthetically deplorable performance. According to Ravenscroft himself, only the "psalms of tribulation" were to be sung "with a low voice and long measure"; the "psalms of rejoicing," he declared, were to be sung with "a loud voice, a swift and jocund measure." [13] Furthermore, the tunes themselves that were in use between 1539 and 1638 (and whose composers are for the most part unknown) were in general characterized by a strength, a grace, and a variety that surpass all but the very best that can be offered by the melodies now in popular use throughout our reformed Christendom. They were mostly modal and possessed an earthy homeliness and a folksong character that would be a welcome relief to the Victorian inanities which retain such an unfortunate grip on the affections of present-day churchgoers. Sir Richard Terry has within the last generation done a great deal of hard pioneer work in reintroducing them to modern parishes, for most of them have not been heard for more than three centuries.

During what one may term the Golden Age of psalm singing, almost every English composer of note tried his hand at harmonizing these tunes. The result is a body of hundreds of little compositions, fascinating to hear today and extremely valuable as documents in the history of the development of harmony.

[12] See p. 31n. [13] Ravenscroft, Preface.

The excellence of the music, however, is unfortunately equalled only by the inferiority of the verses so set and sung. Experiments in translating the psalms into English meter had been made by Sir Thomas Wyatt and by the Earl of Surrey, by Miles Coverdale, by William Hunnis of the Chapel Royal, and by an anonymous journeyman poet whose work appeared in 1549.[14] In the same year appeared the nucleus of what was to be, when complete, the "standard" version of the English rhymed psalter. This was the work of Thomas Sternhold, and it contained nineteen psalms. Before the end of the year a new edition was published containing forty-four, seven of which were by John Hopkins. The Sternhold-Hopkins book became immensely popular. It went through edition after edition, new translations being added from time to time by various hands until 1562, when the work was complete. It contained not only all the psalms, most of them reduced to "common meter," but also a number of "Evangelical Hymns and Spiritual Songs," such as the Lord's Prayer, the Ten Commandments, the Veni Creator, the Creed, and a Prayer to the Holy Ghost, all executed in the same style. As a fair specimen we may quote a couple of stanzas from Psalm 2, done by Sternhold himself:

> Why did the Gentiles tumults raise?
>   what rage was in their braine?
> Why did the Iewish people muse?
>   seeing all is but vaine.
>
> The Kings and Rulers of the earth,
>   conspire and all are bent,
> Against the Lord and Christ his sonne,
>   Which he amongst vs sent.

The tunes to which these verses were sung began to appear in print as early as 1556, when they were published without harmony. Later editions of Sternhold contained also "An In-

---

[14] For a full and compact account of these and subsequent English metrical psalters see Wooldridge (2).

troduction to Learn to Sing," for the benefit of the musically unskilled. In 1563 harmony was provided in the form of 141 compositions, published by John Day in four separate part books. These settings were chiefly the work of Thomas Causton, who provided twenty-seven, and W. Parsons, who did eighty-one; the rest were by Southerton, Brimle, and Hake. In a supplement appeared further compositions by Tallis, Shepherd, and Edwards. Further settings appeared in 1579, 1581, 1585, 1588, and 1591. Thomas East, who had acquired Byrd's patent for publishing music, produced a notable collection in 1592,[15] for which he enlisted the services of ten celebrated composers: John Farmer, George Kirbye, Richard Allison, Giles Farnaby, Edward Blancks, John Dowland, William Cobbold, Edmund Hooper, Edward Johnson, and Michael Cavendish, all well known as madrigalists or lutenists. In 1599 Richard Allison issued a psalter entirely of his own composition, representing the popular style in its purest and most finished state. Thomas Morley, John Bennet, and Farnaby made further contributions to Barley's collection, which appeared some time between 1604 and 1614. In the majority of these settings the tune itself was given to the tenor voice; only in exceptional cases was it assigned to the treble, to which it is invariably given today. Such was the state of psalm-tune composition when Ravenscroft's work appeared.

Thomas Ravenscroft, then in his early thirties and music master at Christ's Hospital, had already proved himself a musician of surprising versatility. His three collections of popular rounds and catches, ranging from religious pieces in Latin to some rather indecorous bits (*Pammelia*, 1609; *Deuteromelia*, 1609; *Melismata*, 1611),[16] were the earliest of their kind,

[15] Edited by Edward F. Rimbault and reprinted for the Musical Antiquarian Society, London, 1844.
[16] The most important and interesting numbers in these three collections were reprinted under the title, *Pammelia and Other Rounds and Catches*, by Thomas

containing for the first time in print the ageless favorite, "Three Blind Mice," as well as the catch, "Hold Thy Peace, Knave," used by Shakespeare in *Twelfth Night*. A few years later, as if to atone for the frivolous character of his previous work, he published a vastly erudite and pedantic theoretical book, in which he deplored the "modernistic" tendencies of his time and pleaded for a return of the complicated medieval systems of time and prolation. By way of illustration, however, he included a few very light and comic madrigals in dialect. His title is interesting: *A Briefe Discourse of the True (but neglected) Use of Charact'ring the Degrees, by Their Perfection, Imperfection and Diminution in Measurable Musicke, against the Common Practise and Custome of These Times. Examples whereof Are Exprest in the Harmony of 4 Voyces, concerning the Pleasure of 5 Usuall Recreations. 1. Hunting. 2. Hawking. 3. Dancing. 4. Drinking. 5. Enamouring.* He had also joined Milton in furnishing anthems to Myriell's *Tristitiae remedium*, and it may have been through this contribution that he first met the scrivener of Bread Street.

Milton, although almost twice Ravenscroft's age, probably found in the younger man a congenial and sympathetic spirit. His musical tastes and affections, formed in the older school, probably inclined him to welcome the plea for ancient order which he read in the *Brief Discourse;* and at the same time his ardent and happy temperament must have relished the bright and frothy elements in Ravenscroft's work. On the other hand, we can never know whether he frowned severely or merely blushed with embarrassment at those catches that smacked rather strongly of the uninhibited manners of the tavern. At any rate, he became a willing contributor when Ravenscroft prepared his *Whole Booke of Psalmes* for publication in 1621.

Ravenscroft, transcribed and edited from the original editions by Peter Warlock, Oxford University Press, 1928.

The Preface.

in Pſalmes, Hymnes and Spirituall ſongs, ſinging with a Grace to the Lord in your hearts.

I haue therefore endeauoured for the fiting of euery heart to that Pſalme, which it ſhall moſt affect, to place ſpeciall Tunes, proper to the nature of each Pſalme, (not imitating Art ſo much, as the naturall inclination, but ioyning one with another,) and am bold to admoniſh the Singers that they obſerue three Rules.

1. *That Pſalmes of Tribulation be ſung with a low voice and long meaſure,* Pſal. 9. 32. 38 51. 102. 130. 143. &c.

2. *That Pſalmes of Thankeſgiuing be ſung with a voice indifferent, neither too loud, nor too ſoft, and with a meaſure neither too ſwift nor too ſlow,* Pſal. 18. 23 27. 30. 31. 46. 48. 66. 81. 104. 105. 111. 118. 122. 124. 126. 138. 144. 145. 146.

3. *That Pſalmes of Reioycing be ſung with a loude voice, a ſwift and iocund meaſure,* Pſal. 33. 34. 47. 84. 95. 96. 98. 99. 108. 113, 117. 135. 136. 145. 147. 148. 150.

In all which, the obſeruing of Time, Tune, and Eare, will produce a perfect Harmony.

Accept kindely, what I haue laboured earneſtly, and vſe it to thy comfort. Thus I end, humbly wiſhing to all true Chriſtian hearts, that ſweet conſolation, in ſinging prayſes vnto God here vpon Earth, as may bring vs hereafter, to beare a part with the Quire of Angels in the Heauens.

Your well according, and

best wiſhing Brother,

Tho: Rauenſcroft.

THE NAMES OF THE
Authors which Compoſed the *Tunes* of the PSALMES into 4. parts.

Thomas Tallis.
John Douland Doctor of Muſicke.
Thomas Morley Bachelar of Muſicke.
Gyles Farnaby Bachelar of Muſicke.
Thomas Tomkins Bachelar of Muſicke.
Iohn Tomkins Bachelar of Muſicke.
Martin Peirſon Bachelar of Muſicke.
William Parſons.
Edmund Hooper.
George Kirby.
Edward Blancks.
Richard Alliſon.
Iohn Farmer.
Michaell Cauendiſh.
Iohn Bennet.
Robert Palmer.
Iohn Milton.
Simon Stubbs.
William Cranford.
William Harriſon.
Thomas Rauenſcroft Bachelar of Muſicke.

A 3

OF

END OF PREFACE AND LIST OF COMPOSERS FROM RAVENSCROFT'S PSALTER

The book is a small one, its pages measuring only about six by four inches, but it contains nearly three hundred pages and is very attractively laid out and printed. Twenty-one composers are represented in it, including (besides Milton) Tallis, Dowland, Morley, Farnaby, Tomkins, Peerson, Parsons, Kirbye, Allison, Farmer, Cavendish, Bennet, and Ravenscroft himself. There is a brief prefatory essay, "Of the praise, Vertue, and Efficacie of the Psalmes," in which the author points out that these compositions may be found suitable for every mood worthy of a Christian, and in which he adds the remark that instruments may add their strength to the performance, "if vocal music be not full enough." There are 105 four-part settings in all, of which seventy-seven make their first appearance here. The tunes, assigned to the tenor throughout, are named after the English cathedral and university towns or after various localities in Scotland and Wales, where they were presumably first popular. In the Index they are classified as English, Northern, Scottish, Welsh, Low Dutch, High Dutch, Italian, French, and Netherlandish. In the body of the book the four parts (cantus, medius, tenor or playnsong, and bassus) are printed separately, with the text of the first stanza of the psalm under each one, the succeeding stanzas appearing without notes. The material is so arranged, however, that all four singers may read their music together and turn the page at the same time.

Milton's best-known contribution appears first on page 62, directly following the heading, "Here beginneth the Northern Tunes." It is a setting of Psalm 27, whose first two stanzas read:

> The Lord is both my health and light,
>   shall man make me dismaid?
> Sith God doth giue me strength and might,
>   why should I be afraid?
>
> While that my foes with all their strength
>   begin with me to braule:

103

And thinke to eate me vp at length,
themselues haue caught the fall.

To the "Tenor or Playnsong" is assigned the "York Tune."
There is a widespread notion that this melody was actually invented by Milton,[17] and it is indeed ironical that this one bit
by which the scrivener is chiefly recognized as a musician is by
no means original with him. He supplied the harmony found
here by writing the parts for the cantus, medius, and bassus, but
the tune itself had already appeared six years earlier in Edinburgh.[18] There, in the Scottish Psalter of 1615, it is called the
"Stilt Tune." Dr. Neil Livingstone, who edited the Scottish
work, in 1864, confessed that the significance of the curious
name, Stilt, mystified him. But Sir Richard Terry, who has
recently produced a monumental edition of this Psalter, has
guessed with convincing insight that we have here an obvious
bit of Scottish humor, for the melody proceeds by wide and
almost grotesque skips, giving the effect of long and ungainly
strides.[19]

Hawkins, in a famous passage, paid tribute to the wide popularity of the tune as it spread through England under its new
name, York, in the seventeenth and eighteenth centuries. "The
tenor part of this tune," he wrote, "is so well known, that within
memory half the nurses in England were used to sing it by
way of lullaby; and the chimes of many country churches have
played it six or eight times in four and twenty hours from time
immemorial." [20] The remark about the nurses sounds a trifle

[17] This notion has been encouraged by many writers who have too readily accepted the statement made by Hawkins (II, 558): "Among the new composed
tunes in this collection, that is to say such as have new or original melodies, the
composition of the author whose name they bear, is that well-known one called
York-tune, as also another called Norwich-tune, to both whereof is prefixed the
name of John Milton; this person was no other than the father of our great poet
of that name."
[18] See Bridge, p. 69; Pulver, p. 328.   [19] Terry (1), pp. 13-15.
[20] Hawkins, II, 502.

curious and has amused several commentators,[21] but the same striding quality that gave the tune its Scottish name might easily be found a fitting accompaniment to the rocking of a cradle. At any rate, the melody has remained in use through all the years, from Ravenscroft's time to the present day,[22] having been moved up from the tenor to the treble or soprano position, and having been given modern harmony and a more rigid rhythm, in accordance with the sad changes in our fashion of singing hymns. As it is now harmonized it appears as a simple tune in a major key, with a clear modulation to the dominant halfway through. It was originally conceived as a modal melody, in the seventh or Mixolydian mode, which is the same as our modern scale and key of G with the seventh or leading tone flattened to an F natural.[23]

Milton of course harmonized it modally, in F, giving an E flat to the medius on the third syllable and in the final cadence in the treble.[24] This feature, as well as the open fifth at the beginning of the second line, gives to the composition that strong antique flavor which sounds at once so curious and so gratifying to modern ears. The B natural in the tune itself at the end of the second line, however, represents a breaking away from the old harmonic manner and an approach to the "classical" rule.

[21] For example, see Bridge, p. 70.

[22] It appeared in the second edition of Ravenscroft in 1633; in Thomas Tomkins's *Musica Deo Sacra* in 1688; in the *Synopsis of Vocal Music* by "A. B. Philo-Mus" in 1680 (with the tune still in the tenor); in W. Gawler's *Divine Harmony* or *Harmonia Sacra* in 1781 (with the tune now in the treble); and in the British Museum Add. MSS. 31420 and 21421. Its latest appearance, so far as the writer knows, is in an arrangement by Geoffrey Shaw in his *Thirty-Six Descants*, Oxford University Press, 1935.

[23] Its mode is indicated by the fact that in Ravenscroft it lies in the scale of F, with two flats in the signature, each one transposing it down a fourth, bringing it to G. Terry (2), p. 2, regards it as in Mode V, the Lydian, but harmonizes it with a flattened leading tone. The question of which mode it actually lies in is purely academic and rather unimportant, since by this time the modern major and minor tonalities had weakened the musicians' sense for the ecclesiastical scales.

[24] Milton's setting is given on p. 196, Example 9.

Thus, as a whole the hymn presents an interesting example of a style midway between the system of the sixteenth century and the conventions of the eighteenth century. It has won the praise of Professor H. E. Wooldridge, who ranks it among the best of all the compositions in Ravenscroft. He rightly holds that psalm composition was already on the decline from the modal purity of the preceding generation, but adds, "Milton's two settings are fine, notwithstanding the occasional use of the degraded cadence, and on the whole worthy of the older school, to which indeed he properly belonged.[25] This same setting of Milton's is again used for Psalm 66, "Ye Men on Earth in God Rejoyce."

For Psalm 138[26] and for "A Prayer to the Holy Ghost" [27] Milton supplied a second setting of the York Tune. Here the harmonization is much closer to the modern major mode, since only one flat appears in the signature, causing the cadences to be characterized by a sharpened leading tone. The second line, with a soaring melody in the treble, is especially thrilling, as are the abrupt modal change of harmony at the beginning of the third line and also the skillful suspension in the medius part at the close.[28] For Psalm 115 the York Tune is again used, this time in a comparatively undistinguished setting by one Simon Stubbs, who had been a contributor to the *Tristitiae remedium*. This setting by another hand would supply further evidence, if it were needed, that the tune itself was not the invention of Milton.

Milton's third and last contribution to the book is a harmonization of a very fine Dorian melody, the "Norwitch Tune," used for Psalms 5, 55, and 102.[29] This one is distinguished

[25] Wooldridge (2), p. 279.   [26] Ravenscroft, pp. 242-243.
[27] *Ibid.*, pp. 266-267.
[28] The second York setting, for the Prayer to the Holy Ghost, is given on pp. 196-197. Example 10.
[29] Ravenscroft, pp. 30-31, 105-107, 174-175.

2 Proue me my God I thee deſire,
   my vvayes to ſearch and try:
As men doe proue their gold vvith fire,
   my raynes and heart eſpie.

3 Thy goodneſſe laid before my face,
   I durſt behold alvvayes:
For of thy truth I tread the trace,
   and vvill doe all my dayes.

4 I doe not luſt to haunt or vſe
   vvith men vvhoſe deeds are vainer
To come in houſe I doe refuſe

vvith the deceitfull traynes

5 I much abhorre the vvicked ſort,
   their deeds I doe deſpiſe:
I doe not once to them reſort
   that hurtfull things deuiſe.

6 My hands I vvaſh, and doe proceed
   in vvorkes to vvalke vpright:
Then to thine altar I make ſpeed
   to offer there in ſight.

7 That I may ſpeak & preach the praiſe
   that doth belong to thee:

Here beginneth the Northern Tunes.

Pſalme 27.   CANTVS.   Iohn Milton.

MILTON'S SETTING OF PSALM 27

2 VVhile that my foes vvith all their
   begin vvith me to braule: (ſtrength
And thinke to eate me vp at length,
   themſelues haue caught the fall.

3 Though they in camp againſt me lie,
   my heart is not afraid:
In battaile plight, if they vvill trie,
   I truſt in God for aide.

4 One thing of God I doe require,
   that he vvill not deuie:
For vvhich I pray and vvill deſire,
   till he to me apply.

5 That I vvithin his holy place
   my life throughout may dvvell:
To ſee the beauty of his face

and vievv his temple vvell.

6 In time of dread he ſhall me hide
   vvithin his place moſt pure:
And keepe me ſecret by his ſide,
   as on a rocke moſt ſure.

7 At length I knovv the Lords good grace
   ſhall make me ſtrong and ſtout:
My foes to ſpoyle and cleane deface,
   that compaſſe me about.

8 Therefore vvithin his houſe vvill I
   giue ſacrifice of praiſe:
VVith Pſalmes and ſongs I vvill apply
   to laud the Lord alvvayes:
      The ſecond part.

9 Lord heare the voyce of requeſt
   for vvhich to thee I call:

Pſalme 28.   CANTVS.   Tho. Rauenſ. B. of M.

Durham Tune.   TENOR, or Playnſong.

And ſo declare hovv vvondrous vvayes,
   thou haſt beene good to me.

3 O Lord thy houſe I loue moſt deare,
   to me it doth excell:
I haue delight and vvould dravv neere
   vvhereas thy grace doth dvvell.

4 O ſhut not vp my ſoule vvith them
   in ſinne that take their fill:
Not yet my ſoule among thoſe men
   that ſeeke much bloud to ſpill. (guile

10 VVhoſe hands are heapt vvith craft &

their life thereof is full:
And their right hand vvith vvrench and
   for bribes doth pluck and pull. (vvile

11 But I in righteouſneſſe entend,
   my time and dayes to ſerue,
Haue mercy Lord and me defend,
   ſo that I doe not ſvverue.

12 My foot is ſtaid for all aſſayes
   it ſtandeth vvell and right:
VVherefore to God vvill I giue praiſe
   in all the peoples ſight.

Pſalme 27.   MEDIVS.   Iohn Milton.

BASSVS.

Haue mercy Lord on me oppreſt,
   and ſend me help vvithall.

10 My heart doth knovvledge vnto thee
   I ſue to haue thy grace:
Then ſeeke my face (ſaiſt thou to me)
   Lord I vvill ſeeke thy face.

11 In vvrath turne not thy ſelfe avvay,
   nor ſuffer me to ſlide:
Thou art my help ſtill to this day,
   be ſtil my God and guide.

12 My parents both their ſonne forſooke
   and caſt me off at large:
And then the Lord himſelfe yet tooke
   of me the care and charge.

13 Teach me O God the vvay to thee

and leadme on forth right:
For feare of ſuch as vvatch for me,
   to trap me if they might.

14 Doe not betake me to the vvill
   of them that be my foes:
For they ſurmiſe againſt me ſtill,
   falſe vvitneſſe to depoſe.

15 My heart vvould faint, but that in me
   this hope is fixed faſt:
The Lord Gods good grace ſhall I ſee,
   in life that aye ſhall laſt.

16 Truſt ſtill in God vvhoſe vvhole thou
   his vvill abide thou muſt: (art
And he ſhall eaſe and ſtrength thy heart,
   if thou in him doe truſt.

Pſalme 28.   MEDIVS.   Tho. Rauenſ. B. of M.

BASSVS.

by an extraordinarily adept—one might almost say inspired—
leading of the three added parts, each one forming an independent melody of surprising smoothness and beauty.[30] It thus
makes a most singable composition, thoroughly delightful to
choirs; but neither Milton's harmonies nor the tune itself ever
achieved anything like the vogue of "York," probably because
of the "minor" Dorian quality which is no longer popular.[31]
The tune has now disappeared from our hymnals. The words,
by Sternhold himself, to certain portions of Psalm 55 ("O God
Giue Eare") are interesting as an example of metrical psalmody of a fairly mean grade: here, for instance, are stanzas 25
and 26:

> But God shall cast them deepe in pit
>   that thirst for bloud alwayes.
> He will no guilefull man permit
>   to liue out halfe his dayes.
>
> Though such be quite destroyd & gon
>   in thee O Lord I trust:
> I shall depend thy grace vpon
>   with all my heart and lust.

Much as the devout English households, such as the Miltons',
enjoyed making pleasant vocal harmony on such verses, the
more sensitive among them could not remain forever satisfied
with Sternhold's "abject" (the word is Professor Wooldridge's)
rhymes. Pleasant as it was to lift up their voices in praise of the
Almighty and His ways, it must have occurred to those who
were endowed with any aesthetic sensibilities that the grand
poetry of David deserved something better by way of metrical
paraphrase. This they undoubtedly felt, even though as good
Puritans they also felt their affections strongly tied up with
the traditions of the revered Sternhold. And indeed Ravens-

---

[30] Milton's setting for Psalm 55 is to be found on p. 197, Example 11.

[31] The tune did appear, however, as late as 1843, in Charles Smith's collection,
Ancient Psalmody (London, Chappell), with the melody in the treble.

croft's work proved to be the very last of the significant treatments of the old version. Not more than two years later the growing dissatisfaction with Sternhold became manifest in the publication of George Wither's superior version of *The Hymns and Songs of the Church*. This was followed in 1628 by a completely fresh metrical translation of the Psalms by George Sandys, son of the Archbishop, with twenty-four new tunes by Henry Lawes. Further versions, all designed to supersede Sternhold, appeared during the reign of Charles I and during the Commonwealth, as the work of Sir William Alexander, Bishop Henry King, Barton, and Rous.

Of particular interest is the fact that the earliest extant works of young John Milton the poet were undoubtedly composed, not only as an expression of interest in the psalm harmonies written by his father and sung with enthusiasm by the family at Bread Street, but also as part of the poetical revolt against Sternhold. These are of course his paraphrases on Psalms 114 and 136, with which he continued to be so pleased that he included them in the 1645 edition of his poems, under the prideful note, "This and the following *Psalm* were done by the Author at fifteen years old." He must have written them, then, some time in 1623, during his last year at St. Paul's and at just about the time when George Wither's *Hymns* appeared.

In Sternhold, Psalm 114 begins as follows:

> When Israel by Gods addresse,
> > from Pharaohs land was bent,
> And Iacobs house the strangers left,
> > and in the same traine went. . . .

This characteristic jingle the boy Milton turned into dignified rhymed couplets in pentameter:

> When the blest seed of Terah's faithful Son,
> After long toil their liberty had won. . . .

It is doubtful whether the young poet ever intended this poem
to be sung, since its metrical form was not adaptable to any of
the tunes in use at the time. Such an intention, however, may
have inspired his version of Psalm 136, with the famous refrain at the close of each verse, of which the Sternhold work
had already provided two paraphrases. Of these, the first made
use of the Authorized and Geneva versions of the refrain, "For
his mercy endureth forever;" the second displayed a more
lively and elaborate scheme:

> O laud the Lord benigne,
> Whose mercies last for aye:
> Giue thanks and praises sing
> To God of Gods I say:
> > *For certainly,*
> > *His mercies dure,*
> > *Both firm and sure,*
> > *Eternally.*

Milton's composition is frankly and almost aggressively metrical:

> Let us with gladsom mind
> Praise the Lord for he is kind,
> > *For his mercies aye endure,*
> > *Ever faithfull, ever sure.*

This is eminently singable; and one cannot help wondering
whether the boy ever offered it to his father for musical setting
and whether the scrivener was moved to supply tune or harmony
for it. The speculation is attractive, but there is no direct evidence of any such collaboration between father and son. Twenty-
five years later the poet was to turn to psalmody again, for in
April of 1648 he rendered Psalms 80 to 88 into the singable
common meter made familiar to him in his youth by Sternhold
and his father. This effect may have been a memorial act of
filial reverence, for it took place almost exactly on the first
anniversary of the scrivener's death.

At any rate, in the year that saw the appearance of Ravenscroft's Psalter, the elder Milton was still vigorously pushing forward his practical affairs. Although he was already approaching his sixtieth year, he now engaged in the first of those extensive operations in London real estate which he is known to have carried on. There still exists a deed, dated May 2, 1621, recording the sale of a piece of property near the north end of Gray's Inn Lane, with its "peece or pcell of ground or garden plott," by one Leonard Poe, a London physician, to John Milton, "Cittizen and Scrivener of London" and John Lane, his old friend the poet,[32] for the sum of 110 pounds and ten shillings.[33]

In the same year, as we learn from the official records of the Scriveners' Company,[34] a certain Richard Milton, son of a Thomas Milton, was admitted to membership in that body. Masson plausibly conjectures that he was a relative of our Miltons. We learn further that he had been a "servant" to the scrivener of Bread Street; and it is interesting to note that a namesake of the poet's grandfather was at one time an inmate of the Spread Eagle household.[35] In 1622 our scrivener was again elected as one of the "assistants" in the Company, to act as coadjutor to the master and the two wardens. This time he seems to have served willingly in that capacity, having overcome the scruples he had felt seven years before.[36] In May of 1623 there was issued from his "shop" a carefully executed parchment document, now in the Public Record Office, recording a transfer of property for some clients. It was witnessed by Thomas Bower and John Hatton, "servants to John Milton scrivener." [37] This Thomas Bower was in the following year ad-

---

[32] See pp. 90-93.   [33] Stevens (2), p. 1.
[34] A transcript of these records is found in a MS in the Bodeleian Library (Rawl. Miscell., 51).   [35] See Masson, I, 338-339 and note.   [36] See pp. 80-81.
[37] The original is in the Public Record Office. According to Masson (I, 62-63), "it is a very neat, carefully penned and carefully drawn parchment, highly creditable to the 'shop' from which it issued."

mitted to the Company and was later to enter into an important and adventurous partnership with Milton.[38]

Late in 1624 the scrivener's daughter, Anne, then between her eighteenth and her twenty-second year, accepted in marriage Edward Phillips, who held a respectable post as assistant to the Clerk of the Crown in the Crown office in Chancery. Here his duties, such as the drawing up of government writs and other official documents, were not unlike those of his father-in-law. His introduction to the Milton household may indeed have come about through some professional contacts with the scrivener. With his usual affection and generosity Milton presented the bride with what the earlier biographers called "a considerable dowry," and the young couple thereupon made a home of their own in a house in the Strand, near Charing Cross.[39] In the same winter, or in the spring of 1624-25, the father had the satisfaction of seeing his boy John complete his work at St. Paul's, and he prepared the poet forthwith for his first sojourn at Cambridge.

Thus, as the scrivener passes from his sixth to his seventh decade, we find him still leading a full and satisfying life, still occupied with his prosperous business, his wholehearted religious devotions, his beloved music, and his thriving family affairs.

[38] See pp. 113, 120, 129-133.   [39] Masson, I, 103-104.

CHAPTER VII

Father and Son

1624-1638

THE YOUNGER John Milton journeyed to Cambridge during the Lenten term of 1624-25 and was admitted to Christ's College on the twelfth day of February. He remained only a week or two on this occasion, his visit being merely for the purpose of having his name enrolled in the books, for choosing his room, and for familiarizing himself with the place.[1] Soon he was back with his father in London, where there was much public excitement over the death of King James, in March, and the accession of the twenty-five-year-old Charles I. He was regularly matriculated, on April 9, as a Lesser Pensioner, and remained at Christ's through the Easter term, which lasted until July 8. In the summer he was again at Bread Street, for the plague was at that time rampant in Cambridge.

During the next seven years he lived the usual life of a university scholar, proceeding to both his bachelor's and master's degrees. We know how he quarreled with his first tutor, William Chappell, and absented himself for a time; how thoroughly he devoted himself to his studies and literary pursuits, and with what brilliant success, so that he gradually won the respect and admiration of his fellow students, who had at first been so offended by his good looks and his reserved demeanor that they nicknamed him the "Lady's of Christ's"; how he was joined at the College by his fifteen-year-old brother Christopher in February of 1630-31.

[1] This is the inference to be drawn from his epistle of March 26 to Thomas Young, his preceptor; quoted in Masson, I, 147-148.

The details of his university career are so well known that their rehearsal in this place may well be omitted. We need merely note that he was frequently in London, especially between terms at Christmas and Easter and during the long summer vacations, so that he could still be considered an active member of the Spread Eagle household. We shall hereafter discuss his activities only in so far as they are directly concerned with those of his father. We must note here, for instance, that his poem, *On the Death of a Fair Infant Dying of a Cough*, was written probably in the winter of 1625-26, since the "fairest flower no sooner blown but blasted" was his own niece, the firstborn of his sister Anne Phillips and the first grandchild of the elder John Milton. The grief elaborately expressed in this early composition was doubtless shared in by the whole family at Bread Street.

Meanwhile the scrivener continued to win recognition as one of the outstanding men in his own profession. Having served as assistant in the Company, he was in 1625 chosen as one of the two stewards, and he seems to have accepted the duties and responsibilities of this higher post. Two years later, at the age of sixty-four, he was elected one of the wardens for the year— a warden occupying the next rank under that of the master himself. But this time he declined the honor. If he was not properly excused, he was fined twenty pounds, that being the penalty required of every elected warden or master who refused to serve.[2] It is possible that he paid this fine very gladly, for he was now rapidly building up a small fortune in real estate and was probably content to take a less active interest in his work as a scrivener. He may already have formed a partnership in the Bread Street shop with Thomas Bower and have permitted the younger man to assume its actual management.

He certainly did engage upon a far more interesting kind of

[2] Masson, I, 339n.

partnership with his son John. In May or June of 1627 the father and son together purchased a piece of property near Covent Garden from one Ann Westrawe, for £358, of which 250 were paid jointly and 108 by the father alone. This property was conveyed to them, according to the deed, "together with all houses edifices buildings shopps cellors chambers romes lightes yardes gardens easements pfittes comodities and apptennces whatsoever to the said mesuage or tente hereby bargained and sold belonging." [3] Dr. David H. Stevens has suggested that the Miltons may have actually resided in the house or houses so described, between 1627 and 1637, perhaps having moved out of the Spread Eagle. But there is no conclusive evidence on this point.

Another deed records that on June 19, 1629, the scrivener sold a "tenement and garden plot" in Aldersgate Street to Alexander Dorington and his wife Mary, for £300. And on July 18, one month later, he purchased from the estate of Sir John Suckling the house on Ludgate Hill in which that gentleman had resided, for £560. Further research may yet bring other transactions to light, but even from the data recently produced it is evident that he disbursed more than one thousand pounds in such dealings within nine years. Thus we can understand quite clearly how he amassed his valuable estate and how he was enabled to provide so handsomely for his children.

Another very curious transaction in which both father and son were engaged took place in 1627. [4] This had to do with the gentleman who was later to become John's father-in-law; he was Richard Powell, Justice of the Peace, of Forest Hill, near Shotover, in Oxfordshire. He had leased an estate and a mansion house and was reputed to be very well-to-do. Forest Hill was less than a mile from Stanton St. John, the scrivener's

---

[3] For details as to this and other real estate transactions of the Miltons see Stevens (2), pp. 1-6, 39-46.

[4] See Masson, II, 492-496.

birthplace, and only four miles from Oxford. It is possible that the elder Milton still maintained some sort of correspondence or other contact with the Oxfordshire branches of his family and with other friends and acquaintances of his boyhood. At any rate, on June 11, Powell, together with a London goldsmith named William Herne, acknowledged that he owed the younger Milton, then an eighteen-year-old university undergraduate, the sum of £500. Masson has conjectured that John may have inherited some property from his grandfather, Richard Milton; that this property was sold to Mr. Powell; and that the £500 note was made in lieu of payment.

At the same time another deed made by the scrivener attested his consent to a nullification of the debt, provided that £312 were paid to John by the following December 12. This payment was not made, and Powell continued to default, since his estate was really in a confused financial condition, which became more desperate as time went on. Eventually he was forced to borrow more money from other sources. For sixteen years the poet held this claim. It was finally settled, after a fashion, by his marriage to one of Mr. Powell's daughters.[5]

Our narrative has now brought us to the year 1630, and it might be interesting to pause here for a brief view of the situation at the Spread Eagle, particularly with regard to the musical activities of the Miltons. The scrivener was in his sixty-seventh year, highly prosperous and certainly as active and gregarious as ever. His good wife was still alive and fifty-eight years of age. His daughter, Anne Phillips, was married and established, and, although bereaved of her first born and destined to become a widow within a year or so, was the mother of two thriving infants, John and Edward. His two sons were both at Christ's College; Christopher as an undergraduate and John as a graduate student.

There must have been many a musical evening at Bread

[5] See pp. 145-146.

Street, especially at those times when the boys and their friends were home from the university. But musical fashions had changed radically, and the old order which the scrivener had so loved had largely passed away. The great age of vocal polyphony in church music and the fine flowering of the madrigalian era were things of the past. The venerable Byrd had been in his grave for seven years. Gibbons, Dowland, Morley, Farnaby, Wilbye, Weelkes, John Bull—all these old masters had passed on. Of the famous *Oriana* composers and of the contributors to the Leighton and Myriell collections, only a small handful, including Pilkington and Nathaniel Giles, survived. Even Ravenscroft did not have much longer to live, for his death has been placed between 1630 and 1635.

With the disappearance of the great composers of the elder Milton's prime, both the technique and the ideals which they had cultivated had given way to newer, more experimental, and quite revolutionary developments. In more senses than one the older system had achieved its heights and had died, and the succeeding system was still groping for that clear expression which it was not destined to achieve until the times of Purcell and of Handel. The ecclesiastical modes were dead; but modern harmony, based on the major and minor scales and keys, had not yet definitely arrived. Unaccompanied vocal music was on the decline, instruments were claiming more and more attention; but a mature, purely instrumental style had not yet been developed. Polyphonic composition, in which each of the many voices or instruments were given melodies of equal importance, was no longer exemplified in anything like its former purity; but the possibilities of real solo "tunes," absorbing most of the listeners' interest and merely supported upon a bass and a few blocks of harmony, had barely begun to be explored. Such tunes, the natural outgrowth of the lutenists' "ayres," formed the mainstay of the masques and embryonic operas which were now attracting most attention. The free and intricate rhythms of the motet and the madrigal were making way for the insistent and unrelieved regularity of dance patterns. The intellectual element, in both composition and appreciation, was becoming steadily weaker. Professional performers, singers in particular, were claiming more and more of the spotlight, at the expense of the former widely diffused amateur spirit, although the era of the public concert was still fifty years away. Finally, composers of English stock had not only fallen under the spell of foreign fashions; they had also personally retired from the field in large numbers, leaving it in the posession of Italian emigrants and Italianate Englishmen.

Under these circumstances one may easily surmise how the scrivener must have felt. He was poised sadly between "two worlds, one dead, the other powerless to be born." Foreign frivolities, in his opinion, were displacing the national traditions which had once seemed so glorious and unshakable. Sincere regret was doubtless mingled with his benevolent interest in the work of the many swarthy newcomers with whom he and his son were now constrained to make music. The most illustrious name among these was that of the third Alfonso Ferrabosco, whose father had collaborated with Ben Jonson, and who had just been allowed a pension of £50 per year as a player of instruments at the Royal Court. Then there was the second Nicholas Lanier, lutenist and masque composer, whose mother had been one of the Galliardello family. There was Theophilus Lupo, one of the many musical Lupos, a violinist at the Court; and several of the Bassanos were still active.

Closely associated with this group were two rising English composers, the brothers William and Henry Lawes. William, already in his late forties, had been a pupil of Coperario, had sung in the choir of Chichester Cathedral and served as a gentleman of the Chapel Royal. Soon he was to compose music for the stage pieces of Davenant and Shirley, and presently he was to find a soldier's death in the Royalist army at Chester. His brother Henry was at this time only thirty-five years old. Also a pupil of Coperario and a member of the Royal Chapel, he was destined to work with both Carew and the young Milton in masques, and also to compose important psalm settings in 1637 and 1648. He was to live through the Revolution, the Commonwealth, and the Protectorate, his last important work being the anthem, "Zadok the Priest," written for the coronation of Charles II. He followed the Italians in developing a kind of "aria parlante" (a compromise between recitative and tune), and his technique bridged the gap between the older vocal fashion and that of Purcell. For this particular style he was to win the tribute of the poet's famous sonnet, *To Mr. H. Lawes, on His Aires.* Although he was the young Milton's senior by thirteen years, a strong friendship sprang up between the two, so that presently, after Lawes had become music master to the children of the Earl of Bridgewater, he was chiefly instrumental in engaging the poet to write the masque of Comus.

Such were the musicians who now forgathered with the Miltons, at the Spread Eagle, at "one Mr. Lawes his house," and in other private homes. Out of deference to the scrivener, those with passable voices would sit around the table, with the well-thumbed part books containing the older madrigals and motets or with Ravenscroft's Psalter, and bring the vocal harmony of the ancient school to life again—thus inspiring the young poet to record his impressions in his *At a Solemn Musick.* At this time, having been affectionately trained by his father, John could probably both sing and play keyboard instruments with some facility. The organ, viols, and other instruments would then be engaged in the "consort," and presently the latest songs and dramatic arias would be heard, in both English and Italian. Among those present there would undoubtedly be Charles Diodati, as an enthusiastic friend and amateur who was at home in both languages.

It was under these genial circumstances that the younger Milton met and was fascinated by the mysterious foreign beauty for whom he penned his Italian sonnets.[6] It seems certain that she was not Leonora Baroni, whom he was to hear several years later in Rome. Her name was probably Emilia; she was a girl of about the poet's age, of Italian parentage, with dark complexion and black eyes. Most important of all, she was an accomplished singer, endowed with a voice that "might lure the toiling moon from the mid hemisphere." So devastating was the impression she made on the twenty-two-year-old poet that he composed four sonnets, together with a *canzone* and one additional sonnet addressed to Charles Diodati, all in her honor. He wrote these in Italian, because it was her language and because she had told him it was the language of love, even though to him it was a *lingua ignota e strana* and although his English companions, "nymphs and amorous swains," had twitted him heartlessly about it all. Emilia's actual identity has thus far eluded investigators, but it seems reasonable to suppose that this dark lady of Milton's sonnets was a daughter of one of the many professional Italian musicians with whom the Lawes brothers, the Miltons, and the Diodatis were consorting at the time. Her last name may have been Ferrabosco, Bassano, Lupo, or Galliardello—and her rather bewitching personality throws a romantic and enigmatic aura over our picture of the musical diversions at Bread Street.

But the time was rapidly coming when the scrivener was to leave the Spread Eagle for good. By 1632, when he was approaching his seventieth year, he had determined to retire from the incessant cares of an active business life and to find a rural

[6] The available evidence as to the identity of this Italian singer is very persuasively set forth by Smart, on whose essay the present account is chiefly based.

retreat where he could pass his old age more serenely. He may already have acquired and lived in a suburban house, but the evidence on that point is still rather confusing. A move into the heart of the countryside, however, now seemed quite feasible. His business partner, Thomas Bower, was fully capable of managing the affairs of the firm, both his sons had practically completed their university careers, and most of his old London friends and associates were no more. The opportunity had at last come to delight in a life *procul negotiis,* although, as we shall see, he was to find himself unable to escape entirely from the pressure of events, exciting, sorrowful, pleasant, and vexatious.

And so he chose for what now seemed to him a final retreat the country parish of Horton in Buckinghamshire, seventeen miles due west of London and a mile from the little village of Colnbrook.[7] Here was luxurious woodland and rich farming country, watered by the Colne and its many tiny tributaries, the entire neighborhood dominated by the distant royal towers of Windsor. The whole parish contained not many more than three hundred souls, including four or five families of gentry, the rest being farmers.

The little church, where the Miltons were to worship during the next six years, dated back to the thirteenth century. It is still standing, although it has suffered some "restoration." It had a square ivy-covered tower; within the main porch was an old Norman arch, under which one entered the nave with its two narrow aisles and chancel. The rectory, nearby, had just been occupied by the Rev. Edward Goodall and his wife Sarah; he had formerly been assistant to Thomas Gataker, of Rotherhithe, a Puritan minister of considerable repute. Now, on his comfortable income of £100 per year, he undertook to guide the spiritual life of his flock. It is impossible to discover how large

[7] For an account of Horton in Milton's time see Masson, I, 337-339, 552-568.

a part music played in his Sunday services, but we may be certain that it was of a modest nature and that there was at least the singing of psalms. On an open tract behind the church was the manor house, inhabited by the well-to-do Bulstrode clan, consisting of the grandfather, Henry, a widower, and his two sons Thomas and Edward, with their families. Here was to be the center of the Miltons' social life outside their own home.

Just what sort of dwelling the retired scrivener acquired is now unfortunately impossible to ascertain. He may have bought the property outright, but it seems more likely that he held it by rent on a lease. Local tradition had it that the edifice stood near the church, with streams of water running through the grounds, and that the younger Milton composed his verses under an old apple tree—but that is the sheerest inventive speculation. All the houses in the neighborhood, with the exception of the church, have now disappeared. Milton's was demolished about 1798, and, although there was still living in 1850 at least one person who could have described it, he was never asked to do so.[8] It has thus been engulfed by hopeless oblivion.

Into this now shadowy and unremembered house Milton moved with his wife before the summer of 1632. His organ and the chest of viols and the virginals and the part books, which had so often provided solace and inspiration of an evening at the Spread Eagle, were carefully packed and transported to the country. His daughter Anne remained in London with her family. His sixteen-year-old son, Christopher, had determined to leave Christ's College, after only two years of residence and without a degree, and to study law in the metropolis; he was duly admitted to the Inner Temple on September 22. Now what was to be the career and position of his son John, who had received his Master's degree and left Cambridge for good in July?

[8] See Masson, I, 560.

121

The solution of this problem was reached after many conversations betwixt father and son, both being quite serious, but affectionate withal. Its record, as found in three of the poet's major works, forms one of the most revealing and admirable episodes in all the Milton annals. It throws a brilliant light on the bold ambitions of the younger and on the sheer sympathy and benevolence of the elder.

We have seen[9] how the scrivener, in providing the boy with the best obtainable classical schooling, had naturally imagined the Church as his logical career. And as time went on and the young man showed an increasing disposition to piety, philosophy, and learning, this intention gradually took on substance as a certainty. But the father herein reckoned without two powerful tendencies in his son's character; tendencies which later on, as now, were to shape his ultimate greatness. These were, first, the revolutionary vigor and independence of his judgments, and second, his colossal aspirations as a creator of poetry. The first tendency had already disposed forever of the possibility of his becoming a churchman. Nine years later, in a bitterly controversial passage in *The Reason of Church Government*, he was to summarize the position which he had taken in this matter, as follows:

The Church, to whose service, by the intentions of my parents and friends, I was destined of a child, and in mine own resolutions till, coming to some maturity of years, and perceiving what tyranny had invaded the Church, that he who would take orders must subscribe slave, and take an oath withal, which unless he took with a conscience that would retch, he must either straight perjure or split his faith,—I thought it better to prefer a blameless silence before the sacred office of speaking bought and begun with servitude and foreswearing. However thus Church-outed by the Prelates, hence may appear the right I have to meddle in these matters. . . .

One can imagine that the father at first felt something akin

[9] See pp. 95-96.

to consternation at such adamantine decision. But apparently he displayed no anger, recalling perhaps the woeful result of his religious differences with his own father so many years ago. Whether he agreed with this radical condemnation of the Established Church practices we do not know. But he was not the parent to force upon his son a course that might create "retchings" of conscience. Very well, then, had John considered another career? The law, perhaps? The answer to this was simple; the legal profession had likewise been contemplated; it had been found shot through with vapidity and trickery; it, too, had been scornfully dismissed.

It was now definitely incumbent upon the young man to come forward and disclose his positive intentions. He did so. He forthwith declared his determination to devote his life to the study and practice of poetry.

Again the father was taken aback. He did not have to remind his son that he was not insensitive to the seductions of the muses, as witness his preoccupation with the noble science of sound and even some certain labored indiscretions with verses of his own, fifteen years ago. But that sort of thing he had always regarded as an adjunct, albeit an important one, to the pursuit of graver interests. Poetry, to his mind was an essential ornament to a full life, but did not its elevation to a position of supreme importance bespeak a certain shallowness or frivolity of mind? Furthermore, how was a poet to live? Was his son intending to compete with the London wits in the degenerate theater, or to attempt to capture the popular fancy with gaudy jingles or sensational prose?

To this argument John responded warmly and at considerable length. He had no desire to appeal to the rabble or to fritter away his energies on trivialities. Let meaner minds so occupy themselves. True poetry was another matter entirely; it was the cultivation of the heavenly gift that had inspired the prophets and the psalmists of Israel, the bards and seers of antiquity, the Christian saints, the choicest of modern spirits. To aspire to carry on the torch, even in a humble way, that had been in the hands of Homer and Virgil, Job and St. John, Dante and Spenser, was no light or frivolous ambition. Careful and prayerful preparation was necessary for such a mission; years of patient study and meditation over the classics, and the beauties and the great truths of nature and divinity. He was only twenty-four, and although his university had lightly made him a Master, he knew that his education had scarcely even begun.

Against such ardent zeal the father, always indulgent, sensible, and susceptible to artistic enthusiasm, could maintain no protracted stubbornness. He might even have permitted himself a smile when confronted with such precocious earnestness. But he was not the one to remain blind to the eminently practical problem that remained. His next remarks probably hinted rather than posed the question of the material maintenance of the scholar and poet. What about money and substance?

Hereupon the poet must have felt a twinge of embarrassment. He reminded his father that there had never been any definite suggestion that a young man trained as a scholar could be expected to enter into business purely for gain; but there had been those operations in real property by which he had been introduced into the world of finance. Could the scrivener have had some idea that his son would devote himself mainly to the increase of the family fortune?

The father quickly disclaimed any such notion. Possibly he might have entertained it some years earlier, visualizing a most agreeable family partnership, but that had been driven from his mind since he had observed the youth's strong bent toward learning. Fortunately the Milton clan was now amply provided with the world's goods. If the young poet wished opportunity and leisure for literary pursuits, the new home at Horton was the obvious answer. To put the matter selfishly, his presence with his aging parents would go far to brighten the long and possibly lonely days that now stretched before them.

So the matter was settled. Only one embarrassment remained. What would be thought and said by friends and acquaintances at this spectacle of a well-equipped youth, the beneficiary of an expensive education, deliberately living as a parasite and a dilettante, mooning over idle fancies day and night? Let them say what they like, concluded John; the backbitings of mean and jealous minds can easily be endured and disdained. His prime emotions were now an overwhelming gratitude and a profound admiration of a father for whose liberality and affection there could never be sufficient recompense.

The discussions between the two John Miltons, here crudely rehearsed, were concluded by the autumn of that year. One of their most interesting immediate results was the composition of the Latin poem *Ad Patrem*, in which the young poet recorded them while they were still fresh in his mind. This poem presents the most eloquent of all surviving tributes to the scrivener, both as a man and as a musician, and is of inestimable biographical value. In the course of its defense of the poetical career occurs the famous passage describing the father's musical activities. It begins:

Nec tu perge precor sacras contemnere Musas

and it ends with the following elevated, even if properly arrogant, sentiment:

Ipse volens Phoebus se dispertire duobus,
Altera dona mihi, dedit altera dona parenti,
Dividuumque Deum genitorque puerque tenemus. [10]

In Cowper's blank verse translation of these hexameters the passage reads:

[10] See Milton, (3), pp. 139-141; Milton (2), pp. 154-157, for the original version of the entire poem; and Milton (1), I, Pt. 1, with prose translation by Charles Knapp, pp. 268-277.

Father and Son

Nor thou persist, I pray thee, still to slight
The sacred Nine, and to imagine vain
And useless, pow'rs, by whom inspir'd, thyself
Art skilful to associate verse with airs
Harmonious, and to give the human voice
A thousand modulations, heir by right
Indisputable of Arion's fame.
Now say, what wonder is it, if a son
Of thine delight in verse, if so conjoined
In close affinity, we sympathize
In social arts, and kindred studies sweet?
Such distribution of himself to us
Was Phoebus' choice; thou hast thy gift, and I
Mine also, and between us we receive,
Father and son, the whole inspiring God. [11]

---

[11] For the complete Cowper version of the poem, see Milton (2), pp. 581-584.
An interesting translation into heroic couplets is to be seen in Burney, III, 135n
as follows:

Nor blame, oh much lov'd sire! the sacred Nine,
Who thee have honour'd with such gifts divine;
Who taught thee how to charm the list'ning throng,
With all the sweetness of a siren's song;
Blending such tones as every breast inflame,
And made thee heir to great Arion's fame.
By blood united, and by kindred arts,
On each Apollo his refulgence darts:
To thee points out the magic pow'r of sound;
To me, the mazes of poetic ground;
And fostered thus, by his parental care,
We equal seem Divinity to share.

Masson, I, 334-337, contributes a further version in English hexameters, in which
the above passage is rendered as follows:

Do not *thou*, I beseech, persist in contemning the Muses,
Thinking them vain and poor, thyself the while to their bounty
Owing thy skill in composing thousands of sounds to the verses
Matching them best, and thy cunning to vary the voice of the singer
Thousands of trilling ways, acknowledged heir of Arion,
Why shouldst thou wonder now if so it has chanced that a poet
Comes to be son of thine, and if, joined in such loving relation,
Each of us follows an art that is kin to the art of the others?
Phoebus himself, proposing a twin bequest of his nature,

Father and Son

In addition to the heartfelt devotion directly expressed in the poem, a subtler tribute is indicated by its very language, versification, and diction. The youth would scarcely have had the impertinence and bad taste to address a Latin epistle to his revered parent, had not that gentleman been able to read the language with ease. It is furthermore couched in an elegance of phraseology and decorated with a treasury of classical allusion which are remarkable even as compared to the young scholar's other Latin poems. Thus its elaborate style, which would be far from easy for a reader imperfectly educated in the ancient Roman authors, brings us the clear message that the scrivener was a thorough and discriminating scholar, as well as a man of sensibility and intelligence.

Years later, in the *Defensio Secunda,* the poet laconically recounted this episode in his career.

At my father's country residence [he wrote] whither he had retired to pass his old age, I, with every advantage of leisure, spent a complete holiday in reading over the Greek and Latin writers; not that but sometimes I exchanged the country for the town, either for the purpose of buying books, or for that of learning anything new in Mathematics or in Music, in which science I then delighted. I . . . passed five years in this manner.

The journey to London was a mere two-hour ride, and could even be accomplished on foot in five hours. Thus John was enabled to maintain his personal, social, and scholarly contacts during his five years of self-imposed rusticity. He visited the Diodatis, the Gills, father and son, who were carrying on an animated literary feud with Ben Jonson, and of course Henry Lawes, from whom he brought back to his father whatever was "new in Music." He made such progress in the art that he

---

Gifted one half to me, with the other gifted my parent,
So that, father and son, we hold the god wholly between us.

A prose translation by Nelson G. McCrea is in Milton (3), pp. 101-103.

eventually was himself able to "compose a song or lesson."[12]

Life at Horton was probably agreeable in every way for the two parents and their son, at least during the first three or four years. The engaging beauties of the neighborhood, the delights of quiet companionship, the zealous cultivation of the arts, which made retirement in the country an almost unadulterated pleasure, soon found their genial expression in *L'Allegro* and *Il Penseroso*. The services at Horton Church itself may have produced the response so eloquently recorded in the latter poem:

> There let the pealing Organ blow,
> To the full voic'd Quire below,
> In Service high, and Anthems cleer,
> As may with sweetness, through mine ear
> Dissolve me into extasies,
> And bring all Heav'n before mine eyes.

And there must have been plenty of music at the Milton house, some provided by John and possibly by a few of his acquaintances, coming down from London, some by the scrivener himself, to the delectation of the neighboring gentry. Airs and dances from the popular masques would alternate with older motets and anthems, psalms, organ voluntaries, and fancies for viols.[13] In his many leisure hours the elder Milton very possibly again produced compositions, both vocal and instrumental, among which it may be permissible to number those interesting works for which no definite date can be assigned and which will be discussed in the next chapter. He undoubtedly took the most lively interest in his son's poetical efforts, particularly in the masque collaborations with Lawes, *Arcades* and *Comus*. But he could not, because of his advancing age, have shared in the

---

[12] Milton (3), p. xxvi. Wood adds the naïve remark that John composed music "by the help of his mathematics."

[13] If Masson is correct in conjecturing that the poet's *At a Solemn Musick* is to be assigned to the year 1633, then that poem may well be a record of a musical foregathering at Horton rather than at Bread Street.

aristocratic connections which these theatrical compositions brought to the younger man, nor could he have taken an active part in the music provided for them, which was of the newer school and thus beyond his more conservative tastes.

He resisted, as far as he could, all attempts that were made to draw him back into the world of business. After he had been settled at Horton for two years, the London scriveners once more tried to inveigle him into an active role in the Company. Probably over his protest, they elected him to their highest office, that of the mastership. It is likely that they intended this action chiefly as a compliment to the most revered and accomplished of their number. But Milton, now over seventy, was firm. He declined to serve, left the mastership to one Charles Yeomans, and his shop in the hands of his younger partner, Thomas Bower. The scriveners may have imposed the statutory fine upon him, but in all probability his excuses were regretfully accepted.[14]

A far more serious and indeed scandalous interruption to his retirement broke over him in 1636. In May of that year an action at law was instituted against the scrivener and his "servant" Bower, flatly charging them with fraudulent malpractice to the extent of £1600.[15] The details of the complaint must have been distressing indeed to the aged *patri, viro integerrimo,* as the poet called him later, accustomed though he was to the merciless methods of court procedure. The instigator of the action was one Sir Thomas Cotton, baronet, of the County of Huntingdon, and his complaint was as follows. His deceased uncle, John Cotton, whom he painted pathetically as "an old decrepit weak man of the age of fourscore years and upwards," had in the year of 1631 delivered to Milton and Bower sums

[14] See Masson, I, 339n.
[15] For a full account of the action, "Cotton *versus* Milton and Bower," see Masson, I, 626-639, 659-661. The present abbreviated narrative is based on the facts which Masson has supplied.

aggregating £3,600, to be let out by them at interest of eight percent, for his benefit. Such a transaction was a legitimate part of a scrivener's activity, and at first all went well. The moneys were loaned to various reliable borrowers, and the interest was regularly delivered to Mr. Cotton.

But after a time, alleged Sir Thomas, Milton and Bower had begun to show the cloven hoof. They refused to bring in either interest or principal, and when poor John Cotton requested reassurance or satisfaction from them, they maintained that the debtors were insolvent and the whole investment in desperate jeopardy. In this perfidy they were aided by one Thomas Holchar, an attorney who was not above such trickery. Furthermore, they bribed one Thomas Colwell, who was then living with Mr. Cotton, with £200, and together with this Judas they so worked upon the feeble mind and timorous disposition of their aged quarry that he was finally brought to agree to a villainous proposal. This came in the form of an offer to buy the debt for the flat sum of £2,000. Old Mr. Cotton, thus victimized, had delivered the bonds to them in return for this amount, giving them a fraudulent profit of £1,600, minus the bribe money. Upon the death of Mr. Cotton, the baronet, as his nephew and executor, had gone to Milton and Bower with this story, and, "in a friendly manner" had asked them to take back their £2,000 and deliver the original £3,600. They had refused, and now he demanded legal satisfaction.

Such was the bill of complaint as it was entered in the Court of Requests. Anxious as the scrivener must have been to preserve his good name and his fortune, he could make no move to do so before the end of the year, since the plague which then afflicted the city made it necessary to adjourn the court at Westminster. Toward the end of the following January, however, processes were served on the two defendants at their place of business in Bread Street. Milton was unable to answer in person, and Bower apparently refused. Both were accordingly held to be in contempt of court, and on February 18 a writ was awarded against Milton by which certain of his goods were to be seized and by which he was to forfeit twenty shillings to the complainant. Bower was treated even more severely; he was not only to forfeit a sum of money but also to be taken into custody and committed to the Fleet prison, there to remain during the pleasure of the court.

Very shortly, however, the court learned that the writ against Milton had been unjustified, since he had been willing at least to answer by attorney. At this point he was materially aided by his younger son Christopher, then a twenty-one-year-old law student, whose action on his father's behalf was officially recorded on April 1, 1637, as follows:

Whereas John Milton, gent., hath been served with his Majesty's process of Privy Seal, issuing forth of this honorable Court, to answer a Bill of Complaint against him exhibited by Sir Thomas Cotton, baronet, plaintiff, Christopher Milton, son of the said defendant, maketh oath that his said father, being aged about 74 years, is not, by reason of his said age and infirmity, able to travel to the City of Westminster, to make his perfect answer to the said Bill, without much prejudice to his health, he living at Horton, in the county of Bucks, about 17 miles distant from the City of Westminster.

Upon receipt of Christopher's affidavit the court granted a dedimus potestatem enabling Milton to have his answer taken at Horton.

The story now turns to the co-defendant, Bower. Whether he was actually incarcerated in the Fleet is not clear, but he did finally appear before the court on April 8. He excused himself for not having answered sooner, pleading illness, pressure of business, and the plague. As to the action itself, he made the following reply. While he had been associated with Mr. Milton, the late John Cotton had indeed turned over to the scrivener, at various times, the sum of £3,600, which had been loaned out in an entirely proper manner. At length, however, the estates of many of the borrowers had declined in value, so that interest had not been forthcoming for as much as two or three years. Furthermore, nearly half the debtors lived in Lancaster and Chester, where they could not easily be sued. Thereupon Mr. Cotton, having become alarmed, offered to assign the entire debt to Mr. Milton, for £1,500. This too generous offer had been declined by the upright man of business.

At this point (Bower continued) the present complainant, Sir Thomas Cotton, having investigated the whole matter, made a word-of-mouth offer in his uncle's behalf to Bower himself, proposing to sell the entire debt for £2,000. Bower accepted this offer in his own private person, as a reasonable business risk. He borrowed £2,000, delivered the same to Mr. Cotton, and received in return all the bonds, with powers to sue and recover. He admitted that the transaction had turned out profitably for him, for he had up to the time of this action "with much travayle" recovered £3,100 of the original £3,600—a clear gain of more than £1,000. But he maintained firmly that there had been nothing shady about the deal. No bribery had been involved, and no pressure upon old Mr. Cotton, and no misrepresentation. Had not Mr. Cotton himself offered the debt to many, including Mr. Milton, for a mere £1,500? Had not the complaining baronet himself persuaded Bower to enter into the transaction? And why had Sir Thomas failed to question its validity during the five remaining years of his uncle's life?

At all events, Bower's testimony helped to clear Milton's position, which was stated at length in a deposition taken at Horton on April 13. Besides a general corroboration of Bower's story, it offered a few additional observations of interest. John Cotton (our scrivener testified) had been "a man of good years," but "of good understanding and memory at the time . . . and able to walk abroad, and did so oftentimes to this defendant's

COURT ORDER EXONERATING MILTON OF CHARGES OF FRAUD

From the British Museum, Cart. Cott. I.5.(5). February 1, 1637/8. The final document in the Cotton lawsuit, establishing the scrivener's innocence. "Primo die ffebruarii Anno R. Caroli decimo tertio./ Whereas Sir Thomas Cotton, Kt., long since . . . and pay to the said defendt. Milton or to his assigne demaundinge the same, the full some of Twenty Shillings of current english money, for his costs herein wrongfully susteyned."

shop in London, and was then no-ways decrepit in body or defective in mind, to his the said defendant's knowledge." Milton, moreover, had no definite recollection of the exact sums involved, "his employment being great that way," but they may have been as alleged.

Cotton, too, out of sheer timorousness, had offered to sell Milton the debts for £2,000 (here the figure does not tally with Bower's) but, Milton declared, he "did utterly refuse, and took it very ill of the said John Cotton that he should make such an offer," both because he would not willingly see a client of his sustain so great a loss and because such a transaction would reflect no credit upon the reliability of his shop. He had assured Mr. Cotton that the debtors were responsible persons and that there was no cause for great alarm. Cotton, however, had persisted in his fears and had entered into some dealings with Thomas Bower, of the precise nature of which Milton was ignorant and to which he had been no party. Wherefore Milton pleaded to be completely exonerated and to be granted "costs and charges in this behalf wrongfully sustained."

To this quite convincing plea the plaintiff's lawyers found it impossible to take exception. During two terms of the court they failed to make reply or to proceed with the prosecution. Accordingly, ten months later, on February 1, 1637-38, a court order declared that as far as Milton was concerned the "matter shall be from henceforth out of this Court clearly and absolutely dismissed forever." The defendant was "discharged of any further attendance in this behalf and licensed to depart at his liberty *sine die*"; finally, he was awarded twenty shillings for "costs wrongfully sustained," the same to be paid by Sir Thomas.

What disposition was finally made of the case against Bower is not known; he persisted in his attitude, holding that his dealings had been completely sound and ethical, but the prosecution continued for some time. Our scrivener, however, now found himself completely cleared. The shadow that had hung over him for two years had been dissipated, and once again his old age seemed free of vexation and anxiety.

But meanwhile his domestic affairs had been charged with heavy sorrow. On April 3, 1637, only two days after Christopher made his sworn statement before the court to the effect that the scrivener's age and infirmity prevented his appearance at Westminster, his charitable wife Sarah died, at Horton. The circumstances of Mrs. Milton's passing are unknown, but there is more than a possibility that her husband's "infirmity" in these sad days was in fact a mental rather than a purely physical affliction. She was at this time about sixty-five years old, for thirty-seven of which she had been his constant companion and solace.

News of her final illness probably brought all of her surviving children to her bedside: John, Anne, and Christopher. Three days later her remains were interred under the chancel of Horton Church, after the divinely simple Burial Service had been read by the Reverend Goodall. Over the grave was placed the plain blue stone, which may still be seen there, bearing the inscription, "Here lyeth the body of Sara Milton, the wife of John Milton, who died the 3rd of April 1637."

The seventy-four-year-old widower contemplated with some ruefulness his own still-vigorous constitution, which was to withstand the rigors of another ten active years. But he was comforted by his children, his grandchildren, and his son-in-law—for Anne after the death of the elder Edward Phillips, in 1631, had married Thomas Agar, also of the Crown Office in Chancery, and had brought him along for the sad occasion. This is indicated by the fact that when the scrivener prepared his defence statement in the Cotton case a week later, the signatures of Thomas and John Agar were affixed to the document as witnesses.

Later in the year the plague struck the Horton neighborhood, the masque of *Comus* was published by Henry Lawes, Edward King was drowned, *Lycidas* was composed, and the younger John Milton began to contemplate a continental journey. He felt that secluded study could add little more to his qualifications as a poet and that unhampered circulation for a time in the great foreign world of living scholarship and art would supply the remaining needs of his education. Again there was discussion between father and son, and again the scrivener's generosity and sympathy were strikingly exhibited. He agreed to the proposal, furnishing the poet with a manservant (as was proper for a learned young gentleman) and financing the entire project, at an expense which could not have amounted to less than £250 per year. Henry Lawes used his influence among the nobility to provide his friend and pupil with the necessary passport.[16]

There was only one serious objection. The widower was now in his seventy-fifth year; was he to be left entirely alone? To this problem his younger son Christopher supplied the solution. He was a youth of twenty-two, was about to be called to the bar, and had already married Thomasine Webber, the daughter of a London citizen. It was arranged that this newly wedded pair were to take up their residence at Horton, to keep the aging father company, at least during John's absence and of course at the father's expense. So the matter was finally arranged. Christopher and Thomasine moved into the country house.

John, in April of 1638, departed for France and Italy, having, as he later wrote, "entreated and obtained my father's consent." And for three years more the elderly scrivener and musician lived quietly on in retirement.

[16] Spaeth, p. 20; Masson, I, 736.

CHAPTER VIII

Remaining Works and Last Years
1638-1647

RETIREMENT, to a mind so alive and vigorous as that of the elder Milton, could never degenerate into stagnation. The eight years which he spent at Horton contributed, as we have seen, their share of trouble and sorrow, as well as less depressing domestic events. But the scrivener must have occupied many a leisure hour with the practice of his beloved music. He took delight in playing the organ, and whenever a congenial group of visitors came to the house, he provided vocal music as well. He had taught his son John not only to master keyboard instruments but also to sing a part in a madrigal or psalm at first sight, as any "complete gentleman" should. The poet had "a delicate, tuneable voice" and "an excellent ear."[1] It was the Milton family's enjoyment of such recreations that undoubtedly prompted the poet to write the familiar lines near the end of *L'Allegro:*

> And ever against eating Cares,
> Lap me in soft *Lydian* Aires
> Married to immortal verse
> Such as the meeting soul may pierce
> In notes, with many a winding bout
> Of lincked sweetness long drawn out,
> With wanton heed, and giddy cunning,
> The melting voice through mazes running;
> Untwisting all the chains that ty
> The hidden soul of harmony.

[1] See Milton (3), p. xxxi; and as Peacham wrote in his *Compleat Gentleman* in 1622, "I desire no more in you than to sing your part sure and at the first sight; withall, to play the same upon your Viol, or the exercise of the Lute, privately to yourself."

Did the scrivener actually compose any more music at Horton? The question cannot be positively answered, but there is very little reason to suppose that his talents in this direction were no longer exercised.[2] He certainly had both inclinations and opportunity. Nothing would be more natural for him at this time than to employ his otherwise vacant hours with his favorite occupation. Now there are extant a number of compositions of his for which there exists no evidence as to date. They might have been produced, so far as we can know, at any time in his career, since his style never underwent any radical alteration or development. It is unlikely that he wrote them after his sojourn in the country, for he was seventy-seven years old when he left Horton. They belong, then, to the Horton period or earlier, and therefore may be conveniently reviewed at this point in our narrative. It is pleasant, too, to imagine that in them he found an exhilaration and comforting escape into the delights of his earlier years.

The first to be considered is a simple and beautiful anthem for four voices, discovered in the library of Christ Church, Oxford,[3] the scene of his boyhood musical experiences. The manuscript in which it appears, in full score with bar lines, dates from the middle of the seventeenth century and contains works by Lupo, Ward, and other celebrated composers of that period. The composition is entitled, "If ye loue me," but no further words are supplied. The present writer has found that the familiar text (John xiv: 15-16) adapts itself to the voice parts very readily.

It is set[4] in the Ionian mode, in C, which accounts for its

---

[2] Aubrey (see Milton [3], p. xxii) states that he "left off" his music "many years before he died." But for this statement there is no persuasive evidence, and the probabilities are otherwise.

[3] Ch. Ch. Mus. MS. 44, ff.52-53. See also pp. 9-10.

[4] Since "If Ye Love Me" has not hitherto been printed, it is now presented in complete form on pp. 198-206, as Example 12. The words, and a few dynamic markings, have been supplied conjecturally by the present writer.

many harmonic effects which visit modern ears in unexpected ways. At the very beginning, for instance, the trebles and tenors seem to establish the "key of G," but a completely unconventional shift in harmony, characteristic of sixteenth-century methods, is effected at the moment when the altos and basses enter. There follows some thrilling part leading, especially through the employment of the device known as "suspension," as the four melodies which comprise the musical material are treated imitatively in succession. The alto part frequently soars above the treble, and the tenor above the alto, while the bass and tenor sustain close intervals by which sharp dissonance melts into the purest triad harmony. An unerring knowledge of the capabilities of the different vocal registers is displayed throughout, as each singer in turn receives an opportunity to display the best qualities of his normal range. Here, if anywhere, is to be found a "linked sweetness long drawn out" and the "untwisting" of the "chains that tie the hidden soul of harmony." The section immediately preceding the *coda* is repeated in its entirety, and near the close there is a remarkable use of the "forbidden" unprepared chord of the second inversion and a "dominant" harmony over a "tonic" organ point.[5] From beginning to end there is sustained a mood of the most intimate and fervent devotion, and it is all managed through the use of the most restrained and economical methods.

What is especially remarkable about this composition is its obvious similarity to Tallis's "If Ye Love Me," which Milton may have sung as a boy chorister. The feeling in both anthems is much the same; the melodic lines used in each are of similar structure. In both there is that appealing kind of voice-leading and voice-crossing by which the texture achieves constant variety, as each strand successively comes to the fore and then sinks away into the main harmonic stream. And in both, the

[5] Note especially the last fifteen measures, on pp. 205-206.

138

principal section is repeated, as if the composer were unwilling to take leave of his meditations. May it not be more than a sentimental fancy to imagine that Milton was here, in his old age, deliberately recreating a musical experience which had in his boyhood so sharply and deeply stirred his imagination?

In another manuscript, also at Christ Church, are found Milton's five remaining compositions.[6] This manuscript consists of six part books and contains both vocal and instrumental music, including "fancies" for viols, an anthem, and a pavan for treble voice with accompaniment, by the second Alfonso Ferrabosco. Four of the Milton pieces found here are "fantazias" for viols in consort. The most interesting, however, is the one entitled "Inomine," written for a single male voice of medium or baritone register and five viols. We have already narrated the colorful traditions according to which Milton composed gigantic "In Nomines" in forty or eighty parts for the light amusement of visiting nobility in Queen Elizabeth's time.[7] It is possible that in the present composition he again sought to recapture the atmosphere of his more lively youth. At any rate, it now becomes necessary for us to examine a little more closely the tradition and the technical form according to which he produced this remarkable work.

The "In Nomine" is one of the as-yet-unsolved mysteries of English musical history.[8] Hundreds of compositions bearing this title are found in manuscripts and printed collections throughout the sixteenth and seventeenth centuries. Every noted English composer from Taverner and Tallis to William Lawes and Purcell produced at least one of these pieces. They were almost invariably written for instruments, usually for viols. None, so far as is known, was produced on the Continent, and

[6] Ch. Ch. Mus. MSS. 423-428.   [7] See pp. 39-41; 66-68.
[8] Wooldridge (1), pp. 461-464. The most comprehensive recent account of the problem is found in E. H. Meyer's article, "The In Nomine," in *Music and Letters*, January, 1936, XVII, No. 1, 25-36.

no one has yet explained why this tradition should have exercised such a powerful and tenacious influence over the English alone. The title itself is something of an enigma. It was spelled in some curious ways: "Innominey," "Inomine," and even "Inno myne." [9] And why "In Nomine"? This might mean that the work was a free imitative composition, a fugue "in name only." But it would seem rather to indicate that the pieces were founded on some particular bit of plainsong from the Latin ritual, even though they were not written for voices. Hawkins[10] pointed to the Introit "In festo sanctissimi nominis Jesu," which begins, "In nomine Jesu omne genu flectatur," and to Psalm 19 in the Vulgate: "et in nomine Dei nostri magnificabimur."

Strangely enough, the "In Nomine" is always based on the same *cantus firmus,* but this cantus has no apparent connection with the title. It is the melody of the first psalm-antiphon of the First Vespers for Trinity Sunday as found in the Sarum Missal. The words with which it is invariably associated are, "Gloria tibi Trinitas aequalis una Deitas et ante omnia saecula, et nunc et in perpetuum." The tune itself is a sturdy old Dorian melody.[11] Upon this plainsong, assigned to one of the parts, the composers exercised all the ingenuity at their command. Sometimes they decorated it with keyboard filigree, as Blitheman did;[12] sometimes, following the example of Taverner, they elaborated the tune with all the known devices of canonic imitation; sometimes they multiplied the number of parts to diabolical proportions, as John Bull and Milton himself were said to have done.

One of the most amusing examples of the "In Nomine" was produced by Orlando Gibbons. It is laid out for four voices and

[9] Van den Borren, p. 162n; Naylor (1), p. 177.

[10] Hawkins, I, 465n.

[11] The "Gloria tibi Trinitas" is presented in unrhythmical modern notation on p. 207, Example 13.

[12] See pp. 10, 13.

five viols. The third viol adheres doggedly to the "Gloria tibi Trinitas," the other strings indulge in free imitation; but the voices, with a complete lack of reverence, give utterance to many of the familiar London street cries, impersonating the town watchmen and the hawkers of turnips, ink, oysters, garters, and sausages, and offering to kill rats or mice, or to amputate "any corns on feet or toes." [13] Such frivolous treatment of ecclesiastical material was not uncommon at the time.

Milton's present "In Nomine" is as curious as any. Here the single vocal part, the tenor, has the usual "Gloria" tune, handled with considerable rhythmic license; but it does not pronounce the words of the "Gloria." Instead, there is found in the manuscript, written under the notes, in an old-fashioned sixteenth-century hand, the following text:

> If that a sinner's sighs, sent from a soul opprest,
> May pierce the firmament and mount the throne
> Where great Jehovah sits, the God of rest,
> Then hear, O Lord, the sad tone of my moan;
> O gracious God, whose goodness gives me light,
> Receive my soul, and prayers in thy sight.

It will be observed that these words are a variation on those which Milton had used for one of his contributions to Leighton's *Teares* in 1614.[14] They may also be a corruption of an anonymous poem set by Byrd in his *Psalms, Sonnets*, etc., of 1588, beginning "If that a sinner's sighs be Angels' food." [15] We seem to have here a double *canis a non canando:* an "In Nomine," using the "Gloria" tune, with totally irrelevant words.

[13] The Gibbons composition is found in several British Museum collections, e.g., Add. MSS. 29372-29377 (Myriell's *Tristitiae*) and 17792-17796. It has been edited for piano and voices by Bridge (Novello's *Part Song Book*, second series, No. 1345.) See also Bridge, *The Old Cryes of London*, Novello, 1921, pp. 40-45. It was performed in New York by the Maganini Chamber Symphony on February 17, 1935.

[14] See p. 77.

[15] *English Madrigal School*, XIV, xxxi-xxxii, 159-164.

The composition itself, however, is of great musical and dramatic effectiveness. The five viols develop the various sections of the tune fugally, first in a grave and restrained fashion, presently in more excited and passionate ways, chiefly by using the devices of shortened note-values and close pursuit, pressing on to a stirring polyphonic climax as the voice soars in fervent declamation. Bold dissonances add poignancy to the subdued conclusion.[16] The whole composition is in Milton's most exalted and emotional vein. One may perhaps legitimately read into it memories of Blitheman and the boy choristers at Christ Church, of the gallant days of Alasco and the great Queen's pageantry, of Leighton's pathetic career and enthusiasms, all interfused with the solemn feelings of a man who has had a life full of quiet triumph, sorrow, and happiness, and who now prepares to face the judgment of his Maker.

The four fantazias for viols, well built and sonorous though they are, must be rated as Milton's least distinguished musical work. They are, in effect, wordless motets or madrigals, displaying but little of the inspiration that a sympathetic text usually provides for a composer of Milton's strength and sensibility. At the same time they show little feeling for the special effects obtainable through the greater agility of stringed instruments. Hundreds of such compositions, "apt for voices and viols," were turned out by Milton's contemporaries, and very few of them, even those of Byrd and Gibbons, are likely to arouse much admiration at the present day.[17] The reason is fairly clear. Before 1630 or thereabouts, English composers had, as a group, developed little capacity for a purely instrumental style, save in

---

[16] On pp. 208-211 (Example 14) are three fragments of the composition, from the beginning, middle, and end.

[17] A large number of these "Fancies" were examined by Dr. Ernest Walker and analyzed in his article, "An Oxford Book of Fancies," in *The Musical Antiquary*, January, 1912.

TENOR PART OF MILTON'S *"IN NOMINE"*

From the Christ Church MS 425, f. 21

their music for the virginals. Their experiments in this direction were still awaiting the touch of genius that was to be provided late in the century by Henry Purcell.

Nevertheless, Milton's fantazias are well above the average quality of his time. The one example in six parts,[18] opening with a fugal development of two subjects simultaneously, has a measure of both charm and dignity, although it sinks presently into something akin to tediousness. The three shorter ones, in five parts, have more to recommend them and may possibly be worth a revival, if only for their historical interest. The one in G, for instance (No. 9 in the manuscript), if taken at a lively tempo, has a considerable rhythmic vitality and a rather fascinating, if conventional, type of imitative polyphony. It might exercise some charm over a modern audience. Five deft string players could make a very joyful noise with this composition and its two companions.[19] But it must be recognized that Milton's claims to musical genius reside ultimately in his vocal works.

Having now reviewed all of the extant works of the scrivener, we may take up the brief chronicle of his remaining span of life.[20] The year 1639 found him still at Horton, a widower, in company with his son Christopher and his daughter-in-law Thomasine. It is possible that he still did a little money lending, but for the most part his retirement was uninterrupted by business. In March of this year Thomasine gave birth to a son, Christopher's first-born; but the infant did not survive long enough to be baptized.

Late in July or early in August, John returned from his continental tour, having been away for a year and three months.

[18] These fantazias are numbered 9, 10, 11, and 22 in the manuscript. Their opening subjects are given on p. 212, Example 15.

[19] A typical passage from No. 9 is printed on p. 212, as Example 16.

[20] Most of the events of the last nine years of Miltcon's life are recorded in Masson: II, 72, 130, 488-496, 508; III, 484-486, 641-643.

He visited the family at Horton several times during the late summer and the autumn, renewing his affectionate companionship with his father. He had already dispatched home from Venice "a chest or two of choice music-books of the best masters flourishing about that time in Italy—namely, Luca Marenzio, Monteverde, Horatio Vecci, Cifra, the Prince of Venosa, and several others." These works, displaying both the older vocal counterpoint and the newer dramatic style of composition, were now eagerly examined and discussed by the father and son.[21]

Before the end of the year John departed for London to undertake the education of the two sons of his sister Anne. These nephews, John and Edward Phillips, were now aged eight and nine. He first took lodgings in St. Bride's Churchyard, in the house of a tailor named Russel; presently he moved into the "pretty garden house" in Aldersgate Street, where there was plenty of space and suburban quietness.

On January 26 of the following year Christopher was called to the Bar of the Inner Temple. On August 11 there was recorded at Horton the baptism of "Sarah, ye daughter of Christopher and Thomasine Milton." Toward the end of the year the family, including the father, now aged seventy-seven, left Horton for good. Christopher had decided to take up his residence and practice his profession at Reading, twenty miles farther away from London. Here, in the parish of St. Laurence, was recorded the baptism of a second grandchild, Anne, on August 27, 1640. But the Miltons remained in Reading for less than three years in all. Public events moved rapidly and tragically, the Civil War breaking out in earnest in 1642. While John, in London, passionately espoused the Puritan cause, Christopher became an active Royalist. This partisanship created an awkward situation when Reading was besieged by the Parliamentarian army in April of 1643.

[21] Spaeth, p. 23; Milton (3), p. xxxv.

The siege lasted only two weeks, the Miltons escaping any injury, and Colonel Fielding surrendered the town to the Earl of Essex. There was no pillage, and permission was granted to all the inhabitants to leave freely within six weeks. Christopher remained for a while longer, but presently took his family away to Exeter. The father, now approaching his eightieth year, naturally wished to keep as far away from the fighting as possible. And since he probably sympathized far more with the Roundheads than with the Cavaliers, he decided to join his older son in London. He was gladly received in Aldersgate Street by the poet, who now found it possible to repay the hospitality he had so amply received in the past.

In the "pretty garden house" the old gentleman was made comfortable enough. He lived there, according to Phillips, "wholly retired to his rest and devotion, without the least trouble imaginable." The household itself was a pleasant, if modest, one. The rooms were very decently, though not luxuriously, furnished—with an organ, among other things, upon which the poet was fond of playing.[22] There was but one servant, Jane Yates. The order of the day consisted chiefly of religious exercises and (in the little school) "hard study and spare diet." Of particular interest to the father were the lessons in singing which John now administered to his nephews.[23]

But an undertone of tension must have been more than faintly perceptible. When the scrivener arrived, late in the summer, John had already completed his swift marriage, his wife Mary had already left the house, and his vexation at being so soon deserted was already mounting. The absent bride was the daughter of the same Richard Powell, of Forest Hill, in Oxfordshire, with whom the Miltons, both father and son, had had some interesting financial dealings as far back as 1627, sixteen years before.[24] The poet's earliest encounters with his young bride

[22] Milton (3), p. xxiv. [23] *Ibid.*, p. xxiii. [24] See pp. 114-115.

probably took place at Forest Hill, whither he had gone in order to make inquiries concerning the large debt which had never been repaid to him. This would explain the otherwise puzzling fact that he associated intimately with an outspokenly Royalist family. He had collected none of the debt, for the Powell estate was already in a financially confused condition, but he returned with the daughter of his debtor. And now, having for the time lost his wife as well, John could not but feel acute exasperation. His father, however, who possibly maintained some amicable connections with the Oxfordshire families he had known in his youth, comforted him as best he could.

The cordial relationship between the two was indirectly reflected in two passages in the poet's principal treatises written in 1644, in which he paid due honor to that art which he had learned from his father. The first is from the tractate *Of Education*,[25] in which he says, speaking of the proper recreation of young students:

The interim of unsweating themselves regularly, and convenient rest before meat, may, both with profit and delight, be taken up in recreating and composing their travailed spirits with the solemn and divine harmonies of music, heard or learned; either whilst the skilful organist plies his grave and fancied descant in lofty fugues, or the whole symphony with artful and unimaginable touches adorn and grace the well-studied chords of some choice composer; sometimes the lute or soft organstop waiting on elegant voices, either to religious, martial, or civil ditties; which, if wise men and prophets be not extremely out, have a great power over dispositions and manners, to smooth and make them gentle from rustic harshness and distempered passions.

The second is a characteristic flight of irony from the *Areopagitica*,[26] exposing the Miltons' extremely liberal and "unpuritanical" appreciation of secular music:

[25] Milton (3), p. 730; Spaeth, p. 111.
[26] Milton (3), p. 740; Spaeth, p. 112.

If we think to regulate printing, thereby to rectify manners, we must regulate all recreations and pastimes, all that is delightful to man. No music must be heard, no song be set or sung, but what is grave and Doric. There must be licensing dancers, that no gesture, motion, or deportment be taught our youth, but what by their allowance shall be thought honest; for such Plato was provided of. It will ask more than the work of twenty licensers to examine all the lutes, the violins, and the guitars in every house; they must not be suffered to prattle as they do, but must be licensed what they may say. And who shall silence all the airs and madrigals that whisper softness in chambers?

The Royalist cause received its fatal blow at Naseby, in 1645, and shortly thereafter the reconciliation was effected between John and his erring young wife. It is not unlikely that the good scrivener was to some extent instrumental in smoothing out the domestic difficulties of his son. In September of this year the united family moved to the larger house in Barbican Street, nearby, a house which was demolished late in the nineteenth century when room had to be made for a city railway. Here John's first child, his daughter Anne, was born on July 29, 1646, a "brave girl," whose advent must have delighted the aged musician, since he now had grandchildren in all three branches of his line. He did not live to see that this granddaughter "grew more and more decrepit" as the years passed.

Shortly after this event the Barbican house received further visitors and residents. Oxford had surrendered in June. Christopher found it expedient to come to the metropolis to enlist his brother's good offices in making his submission to the victorious party. And old Mr. Powell, now overwhelmed by financial disasters which were the consequence both of his incompetence and of his unfortunate political allegiance, was driven to London to rescue what he could of his estate. Before August the ruined man and his wife, together with some of their sons and daughters, had been received by their son-in-law. The household was now presided over by Mrs. Powell. The scrivener again displayed his cordial nature by associating on most friendly terms with his embarrassed relatives. But Mr. Powell did not long survive the wreck of his fortunes. He died on the following New Year's day.

The elder John Milton, too, was approaching the end of his active and honorable life as the Civil War came to its conclusion. He had reached the age of eighty-four in vigorous possession of his faculties. He still read without spectacles. And, as he had lived, always dispensing and seldom demanding personal attentions and sacrifices, so he died, in the spring of 1637, both suddenly and peacefully, and surely "without the least trouble imaginable." He left no troublesome will to cause dissension among his survivors, having without doubt already disposed of his property to everyone's satisfaction. Although his whole estate was at the end "but indifferent," according to Wood, it had manifestly been made so by his generous provisions for his family. The old house in Bread Street passed into John's possession; it was destined to burn down in the Great Fire of 1666.

On March 15 a small procession was formed before the parish church of St. Giles, in Cripplegate, not far from the Barbican residence. The remains of the scrivener and musician were followed by his three children and a company of relatives and friends to the upper end of the chancel. A grave had been opened in the pavement on the right-hand side, and the coffin was lowered. Thirty-seven years later the body of his famous older son, who was now looking on, was to be conveyed to this same resting place. With the final words of the Service, "Blessed are the dead . . . for they rest from their labours," the mourners turned to face a turbulent world, now poorer through the loss of one who had enriched the purest of the arts, and who is to

this day "entitled to a true nobility in the Apostle Paul's Heraldry." [27]

[27] The scrivener was thus characterized by the earliest and anonymous biographer of the poet. See Milton (3), p. xvi. Professor Henry Morley held that a little epitaph penned into a copy of the 1645 edition of Milton's *Poems* and dated October 10, 1647, was the work of the poet himself and was written in memory of the father. But its authenticity has been gravely doubted. See Henry Morley, pp. xxi-xlv, liii, 200; Stevens (1), p. 265, item 2654; Davey, p. 199. The following is a characteristic passage from the disputed tribute.

> Meanwhile the Muses do deplore
> The loss of this their paramour,
> With whom he sported ere the day
> Budded forth its tender ray.
> And now Apollo leaves his lays
> And puts on cypress for his bays;
> The sacred sisters tune their quills
> Only to the blubbering rills,
> And while his doom they think upon
> Make their own tears their Helicon;
> Leaving the two-topt Mount divine
> To turn votaries to his shrine. . . .

List of Milton's Extant Music
AND
Bibliography

Milton's Extant Music—a Chronological List

Works indicated by an asterisk have not heretofore been printed

1601

Madrigal, in *The Triumphs of Oriana*
　1. "Fair Orian," à 6.

1614

Anthems, in Leighton's *The Teares, or Lamentations*
　2. "Thou, God of Might," à 4, with instrumental parts.
　3. "O Had I Wings," à 5.
　4. "O Lord, Behold My Miseries," à 5.
　5. "If That a Sinner's Sighs," à 5.

1616

Motet and Anthems in Myriell's *Tristitiae remedium*
　*6. "Precamur, Sancte Domine," à 6.
　7. "I Am the Resurrection," à 5.
　8. "When David Heard," à 5.
　*9. "O Woe Is Me for Thee," à 5. (Reproduced on pp. 171-189.)
　*10. "How Doth the Holy City," à 6.
　*11. "She Weepeth Continually," à 6.

1621

Psalm Settings in Ravenscroft's *Whole Book of Psalms*
　12. "York Tune," first setting à 4.
　13. "York Tune," second setting à 4.
　14. "Norwich Tune," à 4.

Without date (in Christ Church MSS).
　*16. Anthem, "If Ye Love Me," à 4. (Reproduced on pp. 198-206.)
　*17. In Nomine, for voice and 5 viols.
　*18. Fantazia, for 6 viols.
　*19-21. Three Fantazias, for 5 viols.

Bibliography

ARKWRIGHT

Six Anthems by John Milton; with biographical memoir and note on instrumental accompaniment. . . . Edited by G. E. P. Arkwright. Old English edition, No. xxii. London, Joseph Williams; Oxford, James Parker & Co.; 1900. The memoir is concise and reliable, although it is drawn almost entirely from Masson. The anthems here reprinted are: *Thou, God of Might*; *O Lord, Behold*; *O Had I Wings*; and *I Am the Resurrection*.

BOYCE

Cathedral Music; being a collection in score of the most valuable and useful compositions for that service, by the several English masters of the last two hundred years, the whole selected and carefully revised by the late Dr. William Boyce. . . . Revised, with organ accompaniment, by Vincent Novello. 3 vols. London Sacred Music Warehouses (Novello), 1849.

BRIDGE

Twelve Good Musicians, by Sir Frederick Bridge. London, Kegan Paul, Trench, Trubner & Co. 1920. Chapter vii deals with the elder Milton and contains the result of the author's attempt to discover evidence as to Milton's residence at Oxford.

BUMPUS

A History of English Cathedral Music, 1549-1889, by John S. Bumpus. London, T. Werner Laurie, n. d. 2 vols.

BURNEY

A General History of Music; from the earliest ages to the present period. . . . By Charles Burney. London. Vol. I, 1776; Vol. II, 1782; Vols. III and IV, 1789. An interesting work historically, but thoroughly unreliable. III, 134-136, deals with Milton, and *Thou, God of Might* is printed on p. 139.

Bibliography

CATALOGUE of Manuscript Music in the British Museum
By Augustus Hughes-Hughes. London. Vol. I, 1906; Vol. II, 1908;
Vol. III, 1909. Contains descriptions and tables of contents of MSS
in which many of Milton's extant compositions appear.

CATHEDRAL PRAYER BOOK
The Cathedral Prayer Book, being the Book of Common Prayer,
with the music necessary for the use of Choirs. . . . Edited by Sir
John Stainer and William Russell. London & New York; Novello,
Ewer & Co., and Henry Frowde, Oxford University Press Ware-
house, 1891.

CHAMBERS
The Elizabethan Stage, by E. K. Chambers. 4 vols. Oxford, Clarendon Press, 1923.

COWLING
Music on the Shakespearean Stage, by G. H. Cowling. Cambridge, at
the University Press, 1913.

DAVEY
History of English Music, by Henry Davey. Second edition, London,
J. Curwen & Sons, Ltd., 1921.

DAVIS
Life in Elizabethan Days, by William Stearns Davis. New York &
London, Harper & Brothers, 1930.

ENGLISH MADRIGAL SCHOOL
The English Madrigal School. Edited by the Rev. Edmund Horace
Fellowes. London, Stainer and Bell, Ltd., 36 vols., 1913-1924. Con-
tains both words and music of all the madrigals printed during the
Elizabethan and Jacobean periods. Vol. XXXII is a reprint of *The
Triumphs of Oriana.*

FELLOWES (1)
English Madrigal Composers, by Edmund Horace Fellowes. Oxford,
Clarendon Press, 1921. The most useful review of the subject;
but there is an error on p. 247, where Milton is said to have contributed to East's Psalter; *for* East *read* Ravenscroft.

FELLOWES (2)

English Madrigal Verse, 1588-1632, edited from the original song books, by E. H. Fellowes. Second edition, Oxford, Clarendon Press, 1929.

FELLOWES (3)

William Byrd, by Edmund H. Fellowes. London, Oxford University Press, 1936.

FITZWILLIAM VIRGINAL BOOK

The Fitzwilliam Virginal Book. Edited from the original manuscript, with an introduction and notes, by J. A. Fuller-Maitland and W. Barclay Squire. 2 vols. Leipzig, Breitkopf & Hartel (1899).

FLETCHER

Contributions to a Milton Bibliography, 1800-1930; being a list of addenda to Stevens's Reference Guide to Milton. By Harris Francis Fletcher. The University of Illinois, 1931.

FLOOD

Early Tudor Composers, by W. H. Grattan Flood. Oxford University Press, 1925.

GALPIN

Old English Instruments of Music. Second edition, London, Methuen & Co., Ltd., 1911.

GROVE

Grove's Dictionary of Music and Musicians. Third edition, New York, The Macmillan Co. 5 vols., 1927-1928. The articles on Milton, Psalter, Triumphs of Oriana, Lawes, Leighton, and Ravenscroft are especially useful.

HANFORD

A Milton Handbook, by James Holly Hanford. F. S. Crofts & Co., New York, 1927.

HAWKINS

A General History of the Science and Practice of Music, by Sir John Hawkins. First edition, 1776, 5 vols. New edition, 2 vols., London, Novello, 1875. II, 502-504, deals with Milton, including a reprint of *O Had I Wings*.

Bibliography

HOWES

William Byrd, by Frank Howes. New York, E. P. Dutton & Co., 1928.

JEBB

The Choral Responses and Litanies of the United Church of England and Ireland; collected from authentic sources, by the Rev. John Jebb, A.M., Vol. I, London, George Bell, 1847; Vol. II, London, Robert Cocks & Company, 1857.

LADY NEVELL'S BOOK

My Ladye Nevells Booke. [By] William Byrd, edited, with an introduction and notes, by Hilda Andrews. . . . London and Philadelphia, Curwen, 1926.

LEIGHTON

The Teares or Lamentacions of a Sorrowfull Soule. Composed with musicall ayres and songs, etc. By Sir William Leighton. William Stansby, London, 1614.

MASSON

The Life of John Milton: narrated in connexion with the political, eccesiastical, and literary history of his time. By David Masson. First edition, 5 vols., 1858-1879. Vol. I, second edition, 1881. Index, 1894. London, Macmillan & Company. This work remains the chief source of information on the lives of both John Miltons.

MILTON (1)

The Works of John Milton. Frank A. Patterson, general editor. New York, Columbia University Press. 1931-1938. The first complete critical edition; 18 vols.

MILTON (2)

The Poetical Works of John Milton. Oxford Standard Edition. New York, Oxford University Press, 1935. A convenient one-volume edition of the poems; it contains Cowper's translations of the Latin and Italian pieces.

MILTON (3)

The Student's Milton, being the complete poems of John Milton, with the greater part of his prose works . . . together with new translations into English of his Italian, Latin, and Greek poems. Edited by Frank Allen Patterson, New York, F. S. Crofts & Co., Revised edition, 1934. Contains also a reprint of the earliest, anonymous biography, and of the biographies by Aubrey, Wood, and Phillips.

MORLEY (1)
A Plaine and Easie Introduction to Practicall Musicke, by Thomas Morley. London, 1597. Reprinted in Shakespeare Association Facsimiles, No. 14, Oxford University Press, 1937. The most important contemporary source of information as to the general characteristics of the music of the time.

MORLEY (2)
Madrigales. The Triumphes of Oriana, to 5 and 6 voices . . . 6 part books. Edited by Thomas Este, the assigne of Thomas Morley. London, 1601. Contains Milton's *Fair Orian*.

MORLEY (HENRY)
The King and the Commons. Cavalier and Puritan song, selected and arranged by Henry Morley. London, Sampson Low, Son, and Marston, 1868. Contains the disputed epitaph, supposedly written by the poet in memory of his father.

MORRIS
Contrapuntal Technique in the Sixteenth Century, by R. C. Morris. Oxford, Clarendon Press, 1922. Chapter viii (Some Technical Features of the English School) is a valuable short treatise and contains some examples of Milton's work.

MYRIELL
Tristitiae remedium. Cantiones selectissimae diuersorum tum authorum tum argumentorum labore et manu exaratae Thomae Myriell. A.D. 1616. British Museum, Add. MSS. 29372-29377. Contains ten of Milton's compositions for voices.

NAGEL
Geschichte der Musik in England, von Dr. Willibald Nagel. Strassburg, Trübner. 1. Teil, 1894; 2. Teil, 1897.

NAYLOR (1)
An Elizabethan Virginal Book, by E. W. Naylor. London, J. M.

Dent & Co., New York, Dutton, 1905. A detailed review of the contents of the Fitzwilliam Virginal Book, which contains the work of most of the Elizabethan keyboard composers.

NAYLOR (2)
The Poets and Music, by Edward W. Naylor. London and Toronto, J. M. Dent & Sons, Ltd., 1928. Chap. iii deals with John Milton the poet.

NAYLOR (3)
Shakespeare and Music, by Edward W. Naylor. New edition, London and Toronto, J. M. Dent & Sons, Ltd., New York, Dutton, 1931.

NICHOLS
The Progresses and Public Processions of Queen Elizabeth . . . by John Nichols. New edition, 3 vols., London, John Nichols & Son, 1823. Contains the contemporary accounts of Alasco's visit to Oxford.

PROCTER
A History of the Book of Common Prayer, with a rationale of its offices, by Francis Procter, M.A. Seventh edition, New York, Pott & Amery, 1868.

PULVER
A Biographical Dictionary of Old English Music. London, Kegan Paul, Trench, Trubner & Co., Ltd., 1927.

RAVENSCROFT
The Whole Booke of Psalmes. . . . By Thomas Ravenscroft. For the Company of Stationers: London, 1621. Contains Milton's three psalm settings.

RIMBAULT
The Pianoforte; its origin, progress, and construction. . . . By Edward F. Rimbault, LL.D., London, Robert Cocks & Co., 1860.

RYE
England as Seen by Foreigners, by William Brenchley Rye. London, John Russell Smith, 1865. Contains valuable extracts from Elizabethan accounts, including Hentzner's.

Bibliography

SHAKESPEARE'S ENGLAND

Shakespeare's England, an account of the life and manners of his age. 2 vols. Oxford, Clarendon Press, 1916. Particularly valuable for the study of the elder Milton are the chapters on religion, education and scholarship, and music.

SMART

The Italian Singer in Milton's Sonnets, by John S. Smart. The Musical Antiquary, January, 1913, pp. 91-97.

SMITH

Musica Antiqua, a selection of music of this and other countries, from the commencement of the twelfth to the beginning of the eighteenth century. . . . Selected and arranged by John Stafford Smith. 2 vols. London, Preston. (1812)

SPAETH

Milton's Knowledge of Music; its sources and its significance in his works. By Sigmund Gottfried Spaeth. Princeton, The University Library, 1913.

STEVENS (1)

Reference Guide to Milton, 1800 to the Present Day. By David Harrison Stevens. University of Chicago Press, 1930.

STEVENS (2)

Milton Papers, by David Harrison Stevens. University of Chicago Press, 1927. Some real estate transactions of John Milton and his father, pp. 1-6.

TERRY (1)

A Forgotten Psalter and Other Essays, by Richard Runciman Terry. London, Humphrey Milford, Oxford University Press, 1929. The *York Tune* is discussed on pp. 13-15.

TERRY (2)

Calvin's First Psalter, 1539. Edited, with critical notes and modal harmonies to the melodies, by Sir Richard R. Terry. London, Ernest Benn, Ltd., 1932.

TERRY (3)

The Scottish Psalter of 1635. Edited with modal harmonies, by Richard Runciman Terry. London, Novello, 1935.

Bibliography

THOMPSON
Christ Church (University of Oxford, College Histories), by the
Rev. Henry L. Thompson. London, F. F. Robinson & Co., 1900.

TUDOR CHURCH MUSIC
Tudor Church Music, edited by P. C. Buck, E. H. Fellowes, R. R.
Terry, A. Ramsbotham, S. Townsend Warner. Published for the
Carnegie United Kingdom Trust by the Oxford University Press.
10 vols. 1923-1929. A monumental critical edition of the most im-
portant church music from Taverner to Tomkins.

VAN DEN BORREN
The Sources of Keyboard Music in England, by Charles Van den
Borren. Translated by J. E. Matthew. London, Novello, 1914.

WALKER
A History of Music in England, by Ernest Walker. Second edition,
Oxford University Press, 1924.

WARLOCK (1)
The English Ayre, by Peter Warlock. London, Oxford University
Press, 1926.

WARLOCK (2)
Thomas Whythorne; an unknown Elizabethan composer. Oxford
University Press, 1925.

WEST
Cathedral Organists, by John E. West. London, Novello, new edition, 1921.

WOOLDRIDGE (1)
The Oxford History of Music, Vol. II, the polyphonic period, part 2.
By H. E. Wooldridge. Second edition, Oxford University Press,
1932.

WOOLDRIDGE (2)
Psalter (the English metrical), in Grove, IV, 267-281. By H. E. W.

Music

EXAMPLE 1

CONCLUSION OF MILTON'S MADRIGAL, "FAIR ORIAN"

See page 57

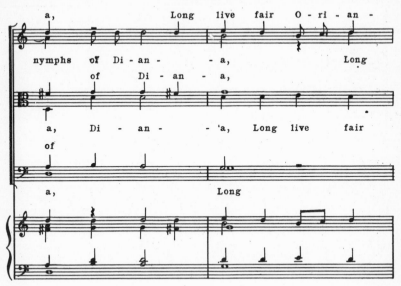

See page 78

EXAMPLE 2

FROM MILTON'S "IF THAT A SINNER'S SIGHS"

See page 78

EXAMPLE 3

FROM MILTON'S "IF THAT A SINNER'S SIGHS"

See page 78

EXAMPLE 4

FROM MILTON'S MOTET, "PRECAMUR"

See page 85

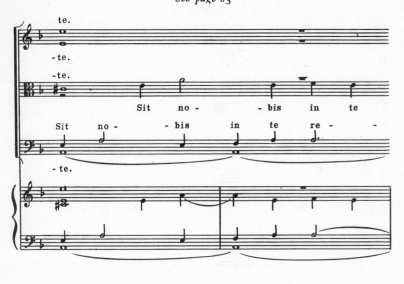

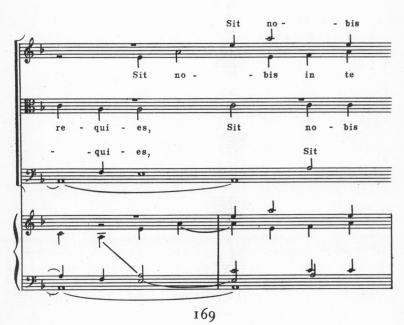

170

EXAMPLE 5

MILTON'S "O WOE IS ME FOR THEE, MY BROTHER JONATHAN," COMPLETE SCORE

See page 88

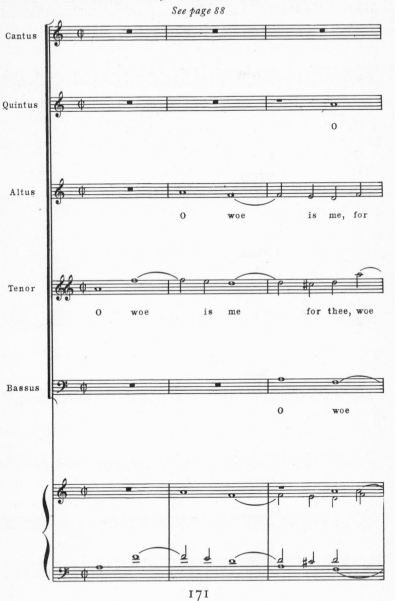

171

173

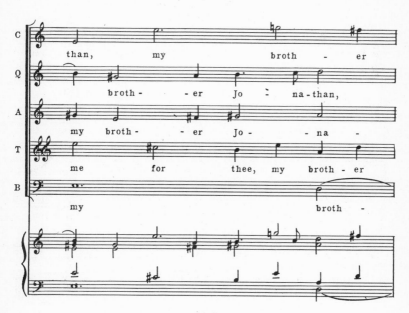

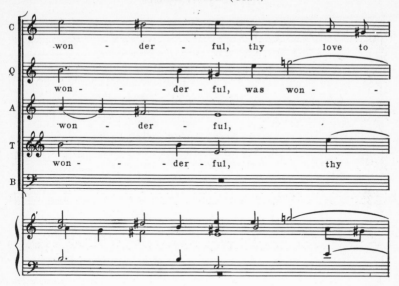

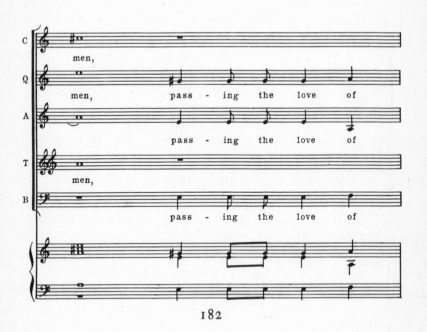

wo - - men, the love
wo - - men, the love of
pass - ing the love of wo - men pass - ing
wo - - men, the love of

of wo - - men,
wo - - - men, and ver - y
the love of wo - men, and ver - y
wo - - - men, and ver - y

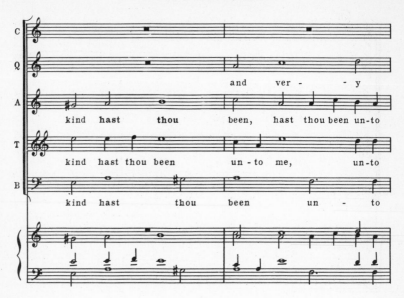

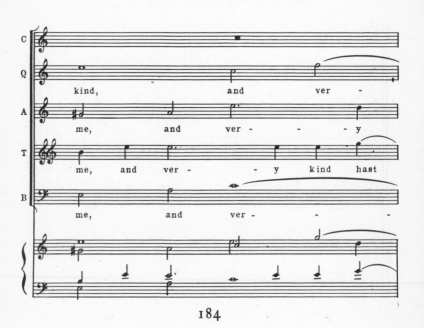

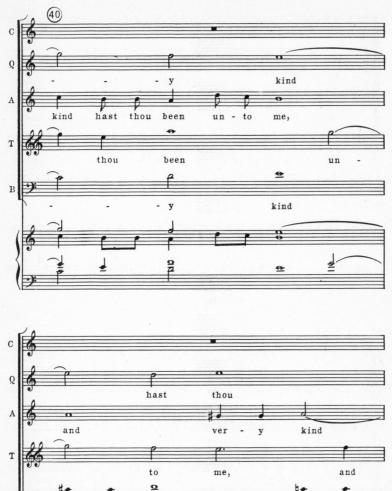

188

189

EXAMPLE 6

FROM MILTON'S "HOW DOTH THE CITY REMAIN SOLITARY"

See page 90

EXAMPLE 7

FROM MILTON'S "HOW DOTH THE CITY REMAIN SOLITARY"

See page 90

EXAMPLE 8

FROM MILTON'S "SHE WEEPETH CONTINUALLY"

See page 90

193

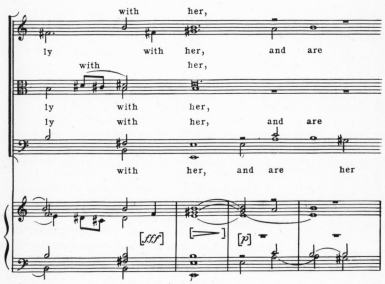

EXAMPLE 9

MILTON'S FIRST SETTING OF THE "YORK" TUNE

See page 105

EXAMPLE 10

MILTON'S SECOND SETTING OF THE "YORK" TUNE

See page 106

Teach us to know thy word a - right,

that we do nev - er fall.

EXAMPLE 11
MILTON'S SETTING OF THE "NORWICH" TUNE
See page 107

Cantus Medius

Tenor or Playnsong Bassus

O God give ear and do ap - ply

to hear me when I pray,

and when to thee I call and cry,

hide not thy face a - way.

EXAMPLE 12

MILTON'S "IF YE LOVE ME," COMPLETE SCORE

See page 137

IF YE LOVE ME (Cont.)

IF YE LOVE ME (Cont.)

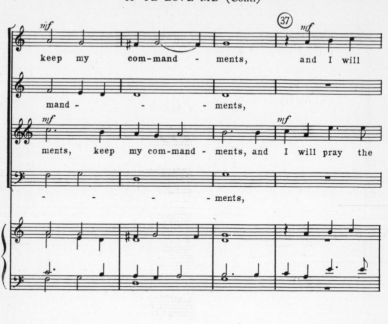

keep my com-mand - ments, and I will

mand - - ments,

ments, keep my com-mand - ments, and I will pray the

- - - - ments,

pray the Fa - ther the Fa - ther, and I will

and I will pray the Fa-ther, I will pray

Fa - ther the Fa - - ther, and I will

and I will pray the Fa -

202

pray the Fa- -ther, and

the Fa-ther, and I will pray, and he shall give

pray the Fa-ther, and I will pray the

ther, and I will pray, and he

he shall give you an - oth -

you an - oth-er com-fort-er, and he shall

Fa - ther, and he shall give

shall give you a com - fort -

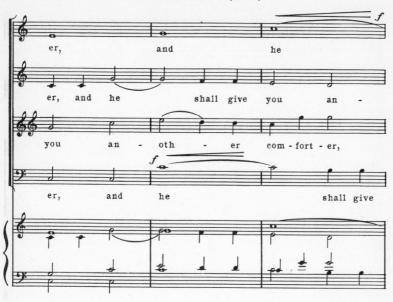

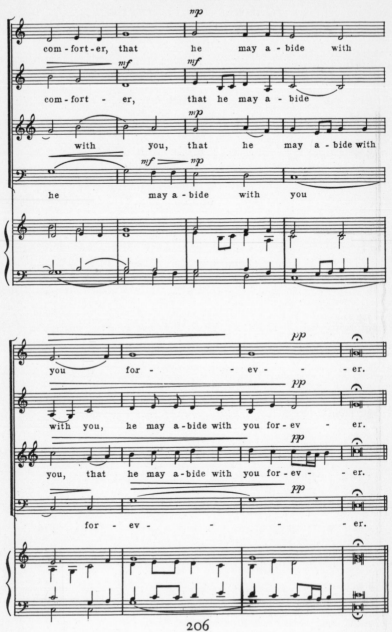

EXAMPLE 13
"GLORIA TIBI TRINITAS"
See page 140

Glo - ri - a ti - - bi

— Tri - ni - - tes ae - qua - -

lis u - na___ De - i - tas

et an - - - - - te om -

ni - a___ sae - cu - - la___

et nunc___ et in per -

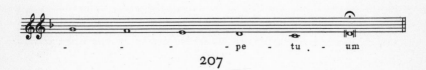

- - - - pe - tu - um

207

EXAMPLE 14
FROM MILTON'S "IN NOMINE"
See page 142

Voice

Strings
(Compressed Score,
with note values
halved)

If

that a sin - - ner's sighs, sent from

a soul op - prest,   etc.

etc.

where   great   Je -

ho -   - vah   sits,

the — God — of

rest, — then — hear,

O, — Lord, — etc. — re - ceive — my

etc.

210

tears and pray - ers in thy

sight, and pray -

ers in thy sight.

EXAMPLE 15
SUBJECTS OF MILTON'S FANTAZIAS FOR VIOLS
See page 143

EXAMPLE 16
FROM MILTON'S FANTAZIA NO. 9
See page 143

Index

Index

Absalom, lamentations for, 86
Actes of the Apostles, The (Tye), 19
Act of Uniformity of 1549, 4n
Ad Patrem (Milton), viii, 96, 125
Agar, John, 134
Agar, Thomas, married to Anne Phillips, 134
Alasco, Albertus: prince, reward to Milton, 34, 39, 41; visit to England, 35; reception at Oxford, 36; forced to flee from creditors, 38
Aldersgate Street, London, Milton's home in, 145
Alexander, Sir William, 108
Allegro, L' (Milton), 128; excerpt, 136
Allhallows parish, London, 51, 68f.
Allison, Richard, psalm tunes, 69, 101, 103
Allwood, Richard, Master, 13
Anthem, superseded motet, 29
Arcades (Milton in collaboration with Lawes), 128
Areopagitica, 146; excerpt, 147
"Aria parlante," 118
Art song, solo, 49
At a Solemn Musick (Milton), viii, 118, 128n
Ayre, 49
Ayres (Bartlett), 62
Ayres (Campion), 62
Ayres (Ferrabosco), 62, 65
Ayres (Pilkington), 62

Baker, Sir Richard, 39
Barbicon Street, London, the Miltons move to, 147
Baroni, Leonora, 119
Bartlett, *Ayres*, 62
Bassano family, 66, 117
Bateson, "In Heaven Lives Oriana," 58
Bearsley, setting for King David's lamentation for Absalom, 87
Beaumont, *Masque for the Inner Temple and Gray's Inn*, 65
Bennet, John, 55, 101, 103

Best, Charles, 74
Bible, versions used, 88
Bishop's Bible, 88
Blancks, Edward, 101
Blitheman, William, 3; as organist, 10; as music teacher, 11, 12n, 15; epitaph, 11n; *In Nomine*, 13
Bolde, William, 52, 81
Book of Common Prayer Noted (Marbeck), 23
Bower, Thomas, 110, 113; Milton's business partner, 120; charged with fraudulent malpractice, 129; to be committed to prison, 131; reply to action, 131; helped to clear Milton's position, 132
Bread Street, London, Milton's home in, 50; see also Spread Eagle
Briefe Discourse of the True Use of Charact'ring the Degrees, A (Ravenscroft), 102
Brimle, settings for psalms, 101
British Museum, Myriell's collection of Jacobean music, 82
Bull, John, 12, 55, 83; composition in eighty parts, 39; astonishing the Court with his virtuosity, 63; contributes to Leighton's *Teares*, 71
———W. Byrd, and O. Gibbons, *Parthenia*, 62
Bulstrode, Edward, 121
Bulstrode, Henry, 121
Bulstrode, Thomas, 121
Burial Service, Milton's setting for opening sentence, 85
Burney, Charles, 40, 74, 86; quoted, 75
Burt, Thomas, 74
Byrd, William, 55, 78, 83; first book of madrigals, 14; Great Service of, 30; ascendancy to leadership in English music, 32, 46; Latin church music, 32; remained a Roman Catholic, 33; *Turbarum voces*, 33; inaugurated outburst of Elizabethan madrigals, 46; *Psalmes, Sonets, & Songs of Sadness and Piety*, also *Songs*

Byrd, William (*Cont.*)
of *Sundrie Natures,* and *Sacrae cantiones,* 47; virginal music, 47; *Gradualia,* also *Psalms, Songs, and Sonnets,* 62; venerated as *homo memorabilis,* 63; contributes to Leighton's *Teares,* 71; hymn set for five voices, 84; Latin Lamentations, 89
——and T. Tallis, granted monopoly for printing and selling music, 31; *cantiones quae ab argumento sacrae vocantur,* 32
——J. Bull, and O. Gibbon, *Parthenia,* 62

Calvinists, originated custom of singing rhymed versions of psalter, 30
Cambridge, Christ's College, *see* Christ's College
Camden, William, 27
Campion, Thomas, 63; *Ayres,* 62
——and N. Giles, masque for marriage of Lord Hayes, 65f.
Canticles: by Thomas Causton, 7; Latin Mass driven out by, 29
Cantiones quae ab argumento sacrae vocantur (Tallis and Byrd), 32
Cardinal's College: founded, 25; suppressed and re-established as Christ Church, 26
Cartwright, Thomas, invective against Romish profanation of church music, 9
Catholic Church, *see* Roman Catholic Church
Catholics, *see* Roman Catholics
Causton, Thomas: canticles, 7; Benedictus, 8; settings for psalms, 101
Cavendish, Michael, 49, 55, 101, 103; "Come, gentle swains," 54
Chappell, William, poet's quarrel with, 112
Cheapside, London, 51
Chicago A Cappella Choir, performed Tallis's motet, 40
Choirmasters, practice of impressing choristers, 19
Choral music, first important collection, 7n
Choristers: at Christ Church, 4-24; practice of impressing, 19, 63
Christ Church, Oxford: early influences which swayed Milton as an artist, 3-24; musical tradition, 25; founded as Cardinal's College, 25; re-established, 26; Milton's compositions discovered in library of, 137, 139
Christe qui lux est et dies (Whyte), 18

Christ's College, Cambridge, poet admitted to, 112
Church music, movement to simplify, 29; *see also* Music
Church of England, high-church party: tendency to retain language and apparatus of Church of Rome in music of, 29; influence in government circles, 68
Church of Rome, *see* Roman Catholic Church
Church service, English, ordered for all churches, 29
Civil War, 144
Clothes worn by Christ Church students, 27
Cobbold, William, 101
Colbron, James, 48
Columbia University, Milton's music presented before English Graduate Union, xi
Colwell, Thomas, 130
"Come, gentle swains" (Cavendish), 54
Company of Mercers, elected pupils for St. Paul's, 97
Composers, English: under spell of foreign fashions, 64, 117; yield to newer homophonic and dramatic styles, 79; little capacity for purely instrumental style, save in music for virginals, 142; *see also* Musicians
Compositions: in forty parts, 34, 39, 40; produced by English musicians, 1590-1620, 62
Comus (Milton in collaboration with Lawes), 128, 135
Consort songs, 71f.
Consorts of recorders or pipes used in plays, 28
Cooke, Edward, 73
Cooper, John (Giovanni Coperario), 83; *Funeral Teares,* 62; instituted fashion of adopting foreign name and composed music for Beaumont's *Masque for The Inner Temple and Gray's Inn,* 65; contributes to Leighton's *Teares,* 71
Cooper, Thomas, 7
Coperario, Giovanni, *see* Cooper, John
Cotton, John, 129
Cotton, Sir Thomas, action against Milton and Bower, 129ff.
Coverdale, Miles, among first to produce metrical psalms, 30, 100
Cowper, William, blank verse translation of *Ad Patrem,* 125

Index

Cranmer, Thomas, 29
Croce, Giovanni, 54, 55, 83

Dance patterns, motet and madrigals making way for, 117
Danyel, John, *Songs*, 62
David, King: lamentation on hearing of death of Absalom, 86; lament for Jonathan, 87
Day, John: *Mornyng and Evenyng Praier*, 9; harmony for psalm tunes published by, 101
Deafe Composer of Tunes, The (Leighton), 70
Deering, Richard, setting for King David's lamentation for Absalom, 87
Defensio Secunda (Milton), 96; excerpt, 127
Delaber, Anthony, 26
De proportionibus musicis (Gaufurius), 17
Descant, art of, 17
Deuteromelia (Ravenscroft), 62, 101
Dining, at Christ Church, 14
Diodati, Charles, 118f., 119; friendship with poet, 97
Diodati, John, 98
Diodati, Philadelphia, 98
Diodati, Theodore, 98
Dodd, William, 81
Dorian melody, The Norwich Tune, Milton's harmonization of, 106
Dorian mode, 17; Tallis's music in, 23
Dorrington, Alexander, 114
Dowland, John, 49, 55, 101, 103; *Third Books of Ayres*, and *Pilgrim's Solace*, 62; *Lachrimae*, 62, 63; contributes to Leighton's *Teares*, 71
"Du Gott der Macht hast mich gestraft" (Milton), 76
Dunstable, John, 82
Dyet, Anthony, 73

East, Michael, setting for King David's lamentation for Absalom, 87
East, Thomas, collection of psalm tunes, 101
Edward VI, 19; *Revised Prayer Book* of, 29
Edwards, Richard, "In Going to My Naked Bed," 21
Elizabeth, Queen: choirmasters of, resort to press-gang methods, 19; attitude toward church music, 29; granted to Tallis and

Byrd monopoly to print and sell music, 31; personal interest in music, 32; "Triumphs of Oriana," a tribute to, 54ff.; permitted singing of psalms, 99
Elizabethan Injunctions, 31
Elizabethan music, *see* Music
Emilia, 119
England, Church of, *see* Church of England
English Graduate Union, Milton's music presented before, xi
Epitaphium Damonis (Milton), 97
"Evangelical Hymns and Spiritual Songs," 100

"Fair Orian," Milton's Oriana piece, 56, 58, 83
Farmer, John, 55, 101, 103
Farnaby, Giles, 49, 55, 101; setting for King David's lamentation for Absalom, 87
Farrant, Richard, 22
Ferrabosco, Alfonso, 46
Ferrabosco, Alfonso, 2d, 83; *Ayres*, 62, 65; influence in the masque, collaboration with Jonson and Inigo Jones, 64; Jonson's tribute to, 64; excerpt, 65n; contributes to Leighton's *Teares*, 71
Ferrabosco, Alfonso, 3d, 117
First Booke of Ayres or Little Short Songs (Morley), 59
Flemish refugee Protestants, psalmody popular among, 31n, 99
Ford, Thomas, *Music of Sundry Kinds*, 62; contributes to Leighton's *Teares*, 71
Funeral Teares (Coperario), 62

Gafori, Franchino, *see* Gaufurius, Franchinus
Gager, William, 27; plays, *Rivales* and *Dido*, 37
Gamut, 15
Gataker, Thomas, 120
Gaufurius, Franchinus, *De proportionibus musicis*, 17
Geneva Bible, 88
Gibbons, Ellis, 55, 63
Gibbons, Orlando, 63, 83; *Madrigals and Motets*, 62; contributes to Leighton's *Teares*, 71; amusing example of "In Nomine," 140
——W. Byrd, and J. Bull, *Parthenia*, 62
Giles, Nathaniel, 63, 83; contributes to

Giles, Nathaniel (*Cont.*)
Leighton's *Teares*, 71
——and T. Campion, masque for marriage of Lord Hayes, 65f.
Gill, Alexander, 97
Gill, Alexander, Jr., 97
Gloria tibi Trinitas, 10, 13, 140
Golden Age of psalm singing, 99
Goodall, Edward, 120
Grace, custom of singing, 14
Gradualia (Byrd), 62
Great Bible, 88
Great Tom, legend, 3
Greenway, Anthony, 25n
Griffiths, Robert, 81

Hake, Edward, settings for psalms, 101
Hakluyt, Richard, 27
Harmon, Sir William, 70
Hatton, John, 110
Hawes, William, 58
Hawkins, Sir John, tribute to Milton's York Tune, 104
Henry VIII, choirmasters of, resort to press-gang methods, 19
Henry Leslie Choir, Tallis's motet performed by, 40
Herne, William, debt to poet, 115
High-church party, *see* Church of England, high-church party
Holchar, Thomas, 130
"Hold Thy Peace, Knave," 102
Hooper, Edmund, 101; contributes to Leighton's *Teares*, 71
Hopkins, John, 30; contribution to English rhymed psalter, 100
Hopton, Arthur, 74
Horton, in Buckinghamshire: chosen as Milton's final retreat, 120; life at, 128
Horton, Church, 120, 128
Howard Charles, Earl of Nottingham, 54; Oriana collection dedicated to, 57
Hue and Cry After Cupid, The, 64
Hume, Tobias, 63; *Musical Humours*, and *Poetical Music*, 62
Humphrey, Lawrence, 25n
Hunnis, William, experiments in translating psalms into English meter, 100
Hymns and Songs of the Church, The (Wither), 108
Hypodorian mode, 17
"If ye love me" (Milton), 137

If Ye Love Me, Keep My Commandments (Tallis), 9, 138
"I Give You a New Commandment" (Shepherd), 18
Impressment of choristers, 19, 63
"In Going to My Naked Bed" (Edwards), 21
In Nomine (Blitheman), 13
In Nomine, a distinctly English form, 40; one of the unsolved mysteries of English musical history, 139ff.; various spellings, 140
In Nomine (Milton), 34, 39, 40, 141-142
Ireland, assessment for establishing English colonists in, 80

James, King, 61
Jansen, Cornelius, portrait of poet, 95
Jeffrey, Ellen, 49; invited to live with the Miltons, 61
Jeffrey, Margaret, 49; married to William Truelove, 61
Jeffrey, Paul, 49
Jeffrey, Sarah, *see* Milton, Sarah (Jeffrey)
Jeremiah, Lamentations of, 88
Johnson, Edward, contributes to East's *Psalter*, 101
Johnson, Robert, contributes to Leighton's *Teares*, 71
Jonathan, lamentations for, 87
Jones, Inigo, collaboration witth Ferrabosco, 64
Jones, Luke, 74
Jones, Peter, 52
Jones, Robert, 49, 55, 63; *Madrigals*, also *Ultimum Vale*, also *Musical Dream* and *Muses' Garden for Delights*, 62; contributes to Leighton's *Teares*, 71
Jonson, Ben: collaboration with Ferrabosco in production of masques, 64; tribute to Ferrabosco, 65n

Kemp, Francis, 81
Keyboard music, early Elizabethan, 13n
Kidnapping of boys for choirs, 19, 63
Kindersley, contributes to Leighton's *Teares*, 71
King, Bishop Henry, 108
King, Edward, 135
Kirbye, George, 101, 103

Lachrimae (Dowland), 62, 63

Lady's of Christ's, poet's nickname, 112
Lamentations: for Absalom, 86; for Jonathan, 87; of Jeremiah, 88; custom of singing in Roman Church, 89
Lane, John: association with Milton, 90, 110; addition to Chaucer's *Squire's Tale*, and Appendix to Lydgate's *Guy, Earl of Warwick*, 91
Lanier, Nicholas, 65
Lanier, Nicholas, 2d, 117
Lant, Bartholomew, 3n
Lawes, Henry, 3n, 65, 117, 135; setting for King David's lamentation for Absalom, 86; psalm tunes, 108; "Zadok the Priest," 118; masque collaborations with poet Milton, 128; published masque of Comus, 135
Lawes, William, 65, 66, 117
Layefield, John, 74
Leighton, William, 69; his *The Tears, or Lamentacions of a Sorrowful Soule* and the musicians who contributed to it, 62, 71 ff., 83; *Vertue Triumphant* and *The Deafe Composer of Tunes*, 70; quoted, 70
Lepton, John, 74
Liber precum ecclesiae cathedralis Christi Oxon, 10
Lily, William, 97
Liturgic music, movement to simplify, 29
Livingstone, Neil, 104
Lollard, Walter, 99
London: Cheapside or West Cheap, 51; Puritanic piety prevalent among citizenry of, 94
Lupo, Theophilus, 117
Lupo, Thomas, 65, 83; contributes to Leighton's *Teares*, 71

Madrigals, 45; English influence, 46; *Musica transalpina*, 46; making way for dance patterns, 117
Madrigals (Jones), 62
Madrigals (Wilbye), 62
Madrigals and Motets (Gibbons), 62
Mann, A. H., choir at London, performed Tallis's motet, 40
Marbeck, John, *Book of Common Prayer Noted*, 23
Marenzio, Luca, 83
Masque for the Inner Temple and Gray's Inn (Beaumont), 65

Masques, 64, 65; Ferrabosco's influence in, 64; solo tunes mainstay of, 116
Mass, Latin, driven out by English canticles, 29
Masson, David, picture of Milton household, 94
Matthews, Tobie, 26, 36
Maurice, Landgrave of Hesse, 66, 67
Melismata (Ravenscroft), 101
Mermaid Tavern, London, 51
Milton, Anne: birth, 61; marriage to Edward Phillips, 111; *see also* Phillips, Anne
Milton, Anne, 2d, 144
Milton, Anne, 3d, 147
Milton, Christopher, 5n; birth, 81; at Christ's College, 112, 115; determined to leave college and to study law, 121; affidavit in behalf of father, quoted, 131; marriage to Thomasine Webber, 135; living with composer at Horton, 143; children, 143, 144; called to Bar of the Inner Temple, 144; move to Reading, 144; a Royalist during Civil War, 144; moved to Exeter, 145; submission to victorious party, 147
Milton John (composer)
   private life: character, personality, vii, viii, 52, 56, 68, 148; relations with poet son, vii, 95, 122ff., 146; in Oxon, 5n; birth, 5n; non-musical schooling, 10; disinherited, 42; romance with Sarah Jeffrey, 49; marriage, 50; home in Bread Street, London, 50 (*see also* Spread Eagle); grant of arms, 52; children, 52, 61, 68, 81; becomes owner of home and of The Rose, 53; interest in religious issues, 68; most familiar with Geneva Bible, 88; friendship with John Lane, 90; only known poetic effort, 91; Masson's picture of household, 94; affection for Puritanic habits and modes of thought, 94; enjoyment of worldly arts, 95; grandchildren, 113, 115, 143, 144, 147; chooses Horton as final retreat, 120; scholarship, 127; life at Horton, 128; interest in son's poetical efforts, 128; death of wife, 134; Christopher and wife come to Horton, 143; move to Reading, 144; decided to join poet in London, 145; home in

Index

Milton, John (composer) (*Cont.*)

Aldersgate Street, 145; death and burial, 148

business life: friendship with Colbron, 48; bound over as scrivener's apprentice, 48; life as apprentice, 49; admitted to freedom of Scriveners' Company, 50; business career, 50ff.; prosperity, 53, 80, 90, 113; elected an assistant in Scriveners' Company, 80, 110; operations in real estate, 110, 113, 114; chosen steward, and later warden, of Scriveners' Company, 113; determined to retire from business life, 119; elected master of Scriveners' Company, declined to serve, 129; charged with fraudulent malpractice, 129; son Christopher's affidavit, 131; position cleared by Bower, 132; matter dismissed forever by court, 133

music: harmonized psalm tunes, did not invent any, vii; contribution to musical publications, viii; a genius in his own right, x; music presented before English Graduate Union at Columbia University, xi; life as a chorister at Christ Church: influences which swayed him as an artist, 3-24; lessons in instrumental playing, 12; instruction in practical music, or theory, 15ff.; remembered as psalmodist, 30; as a musician belonged to school of Byrd, 32; *In Nomine* of forty parts, 34, 39, 40, 139; rewarded gold chain and medal, 34, 39, 41; *In Nomine*, 40; in London, 44-60; obscurity of early years, 44; musical instruments owned, 53; talent recognized, 53; invited to join in Oriana project, 55; Oriana piece his only madrigal preserved, verses used, 56; "Fair Orian," 56, 58, 83; associations with his contemporaries, 61-79; exchange of compositions, 62; association with Italian colony of musicians, 63; never composed according to newer fashion, 64; said to have composed song of eighty parts, 66; version of Bible used for musical compositions, 69; contributions to Leighton's *Teares*, 75, 76; consort song widely known, 75; German translation, 76; setting of

Leighton's paraphrase of verses from Psalm 55, 76; more grave and penitential settings, 77; today sounds surprisingly modern and radical, 79; most mature and powerful works contributed to Myriell's compilation, 82, 83; Latin motet, 83; words used, 84; one of best specimens of polyphonic period, 85; setting of opening sentence of Burial Service, 85; setting for King David's lamentation for Absalom, 87; treatment of David's lament for Jonathan, 87; artistry revealed in anthems with words from Lamentations of Jeremiah, 88; determined to produce vernacular version of Lamentations, 89; divided enthusiasms, 89; contribution to Ravenscroft's *Whole Book of Psalms*, 98, 102ff.; setting of Psalm 27, 103; use of York Tune, 104ff.; use of Norwich Tune, 104n, 106; settings of psalms 5, 55, 66, 102, and 138, 106; setting for "A Prayer to The Holy Ghost," 106; delight in playing organ, 136; Horton period or earlier: anthem, "If ye love me," 137; similarity to Tallis's "If Ye Love Me," 138; "Inomine," 139; use of "Gloria" tune, 141; in his most exalted emotional vein, 142; fantazias for viols, 139, 142, 143; claims to genius reside in vocal works, 143

Milton, John (poet), influence of father, vii; works demand familiarity with composer and his music, viii; lived on intimate terms with music, ix; artistic environment, xi; device on letter seal, 51; birth, 61; influence of home life and Puritanic habits of thought, 94; portrait by Jansen, 95; destined for church career, 95, 122; precocity as a versifier, 96; tributes to his father, 96, 125; schooling at St. Paul's 97; characteristics, 97, 112, 122; friendship with Diodati, 97; work at St. Paul's completed, 111; at Christ's College Cambridge, 112, 115; quarrel with Chappell, 112; debtors, 115; Italian sonnets probably written to Emilia, 119; received Master's degree, 121; churchouted by prelates, 122; aspirations as a creator of poetry, 122, 123; masque collaborations with Lawes, 128; departure for France and Italy, 135; taught to

Index

Milton, John (poet) (*Cont.*)
master keyboard instruments and to sing at first sight, 136; return from Continent, 143; chest of music books, 144; undertakes education of nephews, 144; espoused Puritan cause during Civil War, 144; repays father's hospitality at his home in Aldersgate Street, London, 145; married to Mary Powell and deserted by her, 145; reconciliation with wife, 147; move to Barbican street, where daughter is born, 147; takes his ruined family-in-law into his home, 147; gains possession of Spread Eagle, 148; buried in church of St. Giles, Cripplegate, 148; epitaph attributed to, 149; works: *Ad Patrem*, a tribute to father, viii, 96, 125; *L'Allegro*, 128; excerpt, 136; *Arcades*, 128; *Areopagitica*, 146; excerpt, 147; *At a Solemn Music*, viii, 118, 128n; *Comus*, 128, 135; *Defensio Secunda*, 96; excerpt, 127; *Epitaphium Damonis*, 97; *Of Education*, excerpt, 146; *Il Penseroso*, 128; psalms paraphrased, 108, 109; *The Reason of Church Government*, excerpt, 122; *Samson*, viii; *To Mr. H. Lawes, on His Aires*, 118

Milton, Richard: yeoman, 5, 6, 115; assessment, 33; elected churchwarden, 41; recusancy, 41, 42, 52; fined, 42; disinherited his son, 42

Milton, Richard, 2d, 110

Milton, Sarah (Jeffrey), 49; married to composer, 50; character, 50; death, 134

Milton, Sarah, 2d, 144

Milton, Thomas, 110

Milton, Thomasine, 143

Mixolydian mode, 105

Modes, 17

Moray, John, 74

Morley, Thomas, 49, 53, 83, 101, 103; quoted, 17; books of madrigals, canzonets, and ballets, 47; *A Plain and Easy Introduction to Practical Music*, 49; brought about recognition of Milton's musical talent, 53; England's foremost madrigalist, 54; scheme for "Triumphs of Oriana," 54ff.; invitation to Milton, 55; edited Oriana collection, 57; only contemporary musician who collaborated with Shakespeare, 59; *First Book of Ayres or Little Short Songs*, 59; death,

61; Burial Service, 86

Mornyng and Evenyng Praier (Day), 9

"Mornyng and Evenyng Praier and Communion" (Custon), 7

Motet: superseded by anthem, 29; making way for dance patterns, 117

Mulliner, Thomas, 13

Mundy, John, 55, 63; songs and psalms, 47

Muses' Garden for Delights (Jones), 62

Music: first important collection of choral music, 7n; theory of, 15; dramatic, 28; liturgic and devotional, conflict between old and new, 28; movement to simplify church music, 29; virginal music, of Byrd, 47; domestic, 62; true effect of vocal, cannot be achieved by playing score on piano, 85; no bar lines used, 85n

——, Elizabethan: revival in British Isles, ix; keyboard, 13n; madrigals, 46; spirit of aesthetic adventure in, entering its decline, 79

——, Jacobean, 58, 61; importance of Myriell's collection, 82; composers represented, 83

——, Tudor, 4, 7ff.; practical, theory, 15; scores the marvel and despair of moderns, 18; Byrd's ascendency to leadership in, 32; obscurity, 58; artistic renaissance apparent in, 62; experimental and revolutionary developments, 116

Musical Dream (Jones), 62

Musical Humours (Hume), 62

Musical publications: remarkable stream of, 61; list of principal (1603-14), 62

Music and letters, xi

Musica transalpina (Yonge), 46, 54

Musicians, English: beginning of submission to foreigners which was to stifle native talent, 64, 117; *see also* Composers

——, Italian, in London, 63ff.

Music of Sundry Kinds (Ford), 62

Myriell, Thomas, responsible for one of most important musical compilations of the Jacobean period, 82; composers represented, 83

Newcastle-upon-Tyne Choir, performed Tallis's motet, 40

Norwich Tune, 104n, 106

Notation, 16

Nottingham, Earl of, *see* Howard, Charles

Of Education (Milton), excerpt, 147

On the Death of a Fair Infant Dying of a Cough (Milton), 113

Operas, solo tunes the mainstay of, 116

Organs: pair of, 11n; pipe organs, 13

"Oriana," intended to represent Elizabeth, 54ff.; *see also* "Triumphs of Oriana"

Otto, Prince, 67

Oxford: music lecture founded, 29; reception to Alasco, 36; Milton's early life at Christ Church, *see* Christ Church

Oxon, University of, 5n

Palestrina, 83; Latin polyphonic settings by, adopted in Pontifical Chapel, 89

Pammelia (Ravenscroft), 62, 101

Parry, John, 74

Parsons, W., settings for psalms, 101, 103

Parthenia (Byrd, Bull, and Gibbons), 62

Peele, George, 27; *Rivales* staged by, 37; *Old Wives' Tale*, 45

Peerson, Martin: contributes to Leighton's *Teares*, 71; to Ravenscroft's *Whole Booke of Psalmes*, 102

Penseroso, Il (Milton), 128

Phillips, Anne: children, 113, 115; death of first husband, marriage to Thomas Agar, 134; *see also* Milton, Anne

Phillips, Edward: married to Anne Milton, 111; death, 134

Phillips, Edward, 2d, 34, 115, 144; quoted, 80

Phillips, John, 115, 144

Phrygian mode, 17

Piers, John, 3, 26

Pilgrim's Solace (Dowland), 62

Pilkington: Ayres, 62; contributes to Leighton's *Teares*, 71

Pipe organs, 13

Plague: in Cambridge, 112; at Westminster, 130; at Horton, 134

Plain and Easy Introduction to Practical Music, A (Morley), 49

Plays, 21; music for, 28

Poe, Leonard, 110

Poetical Music (Hume), 62

Polyphonic composition, 116

Powell, Richard: poet's father-in-law, 114, 145; debt to poet, 115; financial troubles, 147; death, 148

Poynte, A (Shepherd), 12

"Prayer to the Holy Ghost, A," Milton's setting to, 106

Professional performers, claim spot-light, 117

Prolation, 16

Proportions, 16

Protestant sects, psalm singing of, 98

Psalmes, Sonets, & Songs of Sadness and Piety (Byrd), 47

Psalmodists, 30

Psalmody, popular among woollen manufacturers, 31n, 99

Psalms: custom of singing rhymed versions of the, 30, 98; sung after Geneva fashion, 31n; Ravenscroft's *Whole Booke of Psalmes*, 66, 98, 102; Milton's setting for 55th Psalm, 76, 106; Golden Age of psalm singing, 99; excellence of music equalled only by inferiority of verses, 100; Sternhold-Hopkins rhymed psalter, 100; Milton's setting for 27th Psalm, 103; for 55th, 66th, 102d, and 138th Psalms, 106; Stubbs's use of York Tune in setting of 115th Psalm, 106; Sandys' metrical translation of, 108; younger Milton's paraphrases on 114th and 136th Psalms, 108; on 80th to 88th Psalms, 109

Psalms, Songs, and Sonnets (Byrd), 62

Psalms of rejoicing, 99

Psalms of tribulation, 99

Psalm tunes, harmonized by Milton, vii

Psalter, *see* Psalms

Purcell, Henry, 32, 143

Puritanic piety prevalent among citizenry of London, 94

Puritans and music, 69

Ramsey, Robert, setting for King David's Lamentation for Absalom, 87

Ravenscroft, Thomas, 83, 116; *Pammelia* and *Deuteromelia*, 62; *Whole Booke of Psalmes*, 66, 98, 102ff.; on singing of psalms, 99; three collections of rounds and catches: *Pommelia, Deuteromelia*, and and *Melismata*, 101; *A Briefe Discourse of the True Use of Charact'ring the Degrees*, 102

Reading: Miltons move to, 144; besieged by Parliamentarian army 144; town surrendered to Earl of Essex, 145

Index

Reason of Church Government, The (Milton), excerpt, 122

Recusants suspected of political treason, 42

Reformers: insist on simplification of liturgic and devotional music, 29; originated custom of singing rhymed versions of psalter, 30

Renaissance, artistic, apparent in music, 62

Revised Prayer Book of Edward VI, services set forth in, ordered for all churches, 29

Rivales (Gager), 37

Roman Catholic Church: conflict over retention of language and ceremony of, in liturgic and devotional music, 29; custom of singing Lamentations, 89

Roman Catholic recusants, suspected of political treason, 42

Roman Catholics in Ireland, England's scheme to subdue, 80

Rose, The, 53

Rosseter, Phillip, 63

Rounds and catches, Ravenscroft's collections of, 101

Roylist cause defeated, 147

Royal Letters Patent of 1560, 4n

Sacrae cantiones (Byrd), 47

St. Frideswide's Cathedral Church, 3, 26

St. Giles, church of: Cripplegate, composer and poet buried in, 148; epitaph attributed to son, 149

St. Mildred the Virgin, parish church, London, 51

St. Paul's Cathedral School of, 97

Samson (Milton), viii

Sandys, George, metrical translation of the Psalms, 108

Scholes, Percy, 69

Scottish Psalter of 1615, 104

Scriveners' Company, 48, 110; composer admitted to freedom of, 50; assessed for establishment of English colonists in Ireland opposed, 80; composer elected an assistant in, 80, 110; charter granted to, 81; Milton chosen steward, later elected a warden, 113; elected master, 129

Scriveners' Corporation, arms, 51

Segar, Sir William, 52

Service, English, ordered for all churches, 29

Servitors at Christ Church, 34

Shakespeare: interest in music, ix, 60; reference to music in works of, ix, 15, 17, 22, 31n, 59, 102; early years in London, 44; Morley the only contemporary musician who collaborated with, 59

Shepherd, John: *A Poynte,* 12; "I Give You a New Commandment," 18; admonished for kidnapping boys for choir, 19; settings for psalms, 101

Sidney, Philip, 27, 31

Singers, claim spotlight, 117

Solo art song, *see* Art song

Solo tunes, mainstay of the masques and embryonic operas, 116

Songs, consort, instrumental accompaniment, 71f.

Songs (Danyel), 62

Songs of Sundrie Natures (Byrd), 47

Southerton, setting for psalms, 101

Spem in alium (Tallis), 32

Sports, 22

Spread Eagle: Milton's London home, 51; destroyed by fire, 52, 148; musical activities, 115ff.; passed into poet's possession, 148

Spur money, 15

Stansby, William, 72

Sternhold, Thomas, 30; standard version of English rhymed psalter, 100; stanzas from 2d Psalm, 100; words to certain portions of 55th Psalm, 107; paraphrase on 114th Psalm, 108; growing dissatisfaction with, 108

Stevens, David H., 114

Stilt Tune, 104

Stocke, Richard, 69

Stow, John, 50

Stubbs, Simon, used York Tune in setting of Psalm 115, 106

Sturtevant, Simon, 74

Suckling, Sir John, 114

Surrey, Earl of, among first to produce metrical psalms, 30, 100

Tallis, Thomas, 83, 103; harmonies contrived by, 4; *If Ye Love Me,* 9, 138; Dorian Service, 23; and Byrd granted monopoly for printing and selling music, 31; *cantiones quae ab argumento sacrae vocantur,* 32; *Spem in alium,* 32; forty-part motet, 40; Latin Lamentations, 89; settings for psalms, 101

Index

Taverner, John, 25

Teares (Leighton), 62, 71ff., 83

Terry, Sir Richard, 104; reintroduced old psalm tunes to modern parishes, 99

Third Books of Ayres (Dowland), 62

Thornton, Thomas, 27

"Three Blind Mice," 102

Time, 16

To Mr. H. Lawes, on His Aires (Milton), 118

To My Excellent Friend Alfonso Ferrabosco (Jonson), 64-65

Tomkins, Thomas, 55, 82, 103; setting for King David's lamentation for Absalom, 86

Trionfo di Dori, Il, 54

Triton's Trumpet to the Twelve Months, Husbanded nd Moralized (Lane), 92

"Triumphs of Oriana," 54ff.; contributors, 55; Milton invited to join in, 56; made ready for publication, 57; vogue in modern times, 58

Tudor music, *see* Music, Tudor

Turbarum voces (Byrd), 33

Tye, Christopher, 18, 83; *The Actes of the Apostles*, 19

Ultimum Vale (Jones), 62

Vautor, Thomas, *Songs of Divers Airs*, 58

Vertue Triumphant (Leighton), 70

Virginal music, of Byrd, 47

Volpone (Jonson), 64

Wagner, Richard, *Tristan* prelude foreshadowed by Milton, 88

Ward, John, contributes to Leighton's *Teares*, 71

Webber, Thomasine, marriage to Christopher Milton, 135

Weelkes, Thomas, 49, 55, 83; "As Vesta was from Latmos hill descending," 57; contributes to Leighton's *Teares*, 71; setting for 56th Psalm, 78; setting for King David's lamentation for Absalom, 86

West Cheap, London, 51

Westfailing, Doctor, 36

Whole Booke of Psalms (Ravenscroft), 66, 98, 102ff.

Whyte, Robert, *Christe qui lux est et dies*, 18, 84; Latin Lamentations, 89

Whythorne, Thomas, graces, 14

Wilbye, 49, 55, 83; *Madrigals*, 62; contributes to Leighton's *Teares*, 71

Wither, George, *The Hymns and Songs of the church*, 108

Wolsey, Cardinal, 25

Wood, Anthony, quoted, 35

Wooldridge, H. E., 106

Woolen Manufacturers, psalmody popular among, 31n, 99

Wren, Sir Christopher, Tom Tower built by, 3n

"Writers of the Court Letter of the City of London," 81

Wyatt, Sir Thomas, among first to produce metrical psalms, 30, 100

Wynkyn de Worde, 14

Yates, Jane, 145

Yeomans, Charles, 129

Yeomen, backbone of British society, 5

Yonge, Nicholas, 63; collector of madrigals, 45; *Musica transalpina*, 46

York, Tune, 104ff.

Young, Thomas, 96

"Zadok the Priest" (H. Lawes), 118